CANTERBURY TALES

NOTES

including
- *Biographical and Historical Introduction*
- *Chaucer's Language*
- *Summaries and Commentaries*
- *Principal Characters*
- *Critical Analysis*
- *Questions for Examination and Review*
- *Select Bibliography*

by
Bruce Nicoll
University of Nebraska

INCORPORATED

LINCOLN, NEBRASKA 68501

Editor

Gary Carey, M.A.
University of Colorado

Consulting Editor

James L. Roberts, Ph.D.
Department of English
University of Nebraska

ISBN 0-8220-0292-2
© Copyright 1964
by
C. K. Hillegass
All Rights Reserved
Printed in U.S.A.

1991 Printing

Cliffs Notes, Inc. • Lincoln, Nebraska

CONTENTS

CHRONOLOGY OF CHAUCER'S
LIFE AND WORKS

1340 — Chaucer born in London.

1357 — Became page to Countess of Ulster.

1359 — Captured by French while serving in English army and later ransomed.

(1360-72?) — Completed translation of *Roman de la Rose,* and wrote *The Book of the Duchess* and *Legend of Good Women.*

1374 — Became controller of customs in London.

(1374-1380?) — Completed *The House of Fame, Parliament of Fowls,* and several of the *Canterbury Tales.*

1386 — Appointed Knight of the Shire and became member of Parliament; Richard II removed him for his customs offices.

(1380-1390) — Translated *Troilus and Criseyde* and resumed work on the *Canterbury Tales.*

1390 — Appointed Clerk of King's Works at Windsor.

1399 — Pension increased by Henry IV.

(1390-1399) — Completed *Treatise on the Astrolabe, Envoy to Scogan, Envoy to Bukton,* and *To His Empty Purse.*

1400 — Chaucer died and buried in Westminster Abbey.

GEOFFREY CHAUCER
A SKETCH OF HIS LIFE AND TIMES

England in the fourteenth century had a population of about 2,500,000. London was the capital city which a contemporary writer described as "lean, white, and small," encompassing an area of about one square mile.

The English countryside was dotted with small market towns seldom populated by more than 150 persons, monasteries, churches, and manor houses. Between these landmarks were open fields and in some instances native forests. Travel was common and not too difficult because the cities were connected by stone-paved highways constructed during Roman times.

England, in Chaucer's time, was a nation in social ferment. Medieval ism still was a dominant influence in the lives of Englishmen, but the renais sance had assumed definite form and the country stood on the threshold o the modern world. These were the forces which stood face to face: th medievalist believed in the spiritual and the abstract, that the community not the individual, was the great ideal. Man, the medievalist asserted, ha no right to think for himself or to make judgments, for man was a member o a great spiritual community, the church catholic and universal. The earl renaissance man believed in developing his own social groups, and nationa interests, as opposed to a united Christendom.

In Chaucer's time there were many manifestations of rebellion agains the old order of things. Wycliffe and his followers were sowing the seeds o the Protestant Reformation which placed the emphasis on the individua Chaucer's countrymen began thinking of themselves as Englishmen, an national patriotism showed in the battles with France which ushered i the Hundred Years' War. The growth of manufacturing and commerc gave rise to a middle class which speeded the end of the feudal system. Th people demanded more voice in the affairs of their government. The churc became corrupt; this corruption in turn invited corruption among th people. And, in the midst of this social ferment, England was three time swept by the Black Plague which reduced its population by one half an dealt an almost mortal blow to its industry.

This great century of social, political, literary, and religious fermen was nearly half over when Geoffrey Chaucer was born in 1340. His fathe was a successful wine maker in London, and his mother, Agnes de Comp ton, a member of the Court. Chaucer was sent to the Inner Court at St Paul's Almonry where he received an excellent education.

In 1357 Chaucer became page to the Countess of Ulster; he met som of the greatest men in England, among them John of Gaunt, Duke of Lan caster. Two years later Chaucer, as a soldier, went to France on an inva sion excursion which was doomed to failure. He was captured, and in 136 was successfully ransomed. No information is available about Chaucer agai until 1366. By that time Chaucer's father was dead, his mother was re married, and Chaucer was married to a woman named Philippa de Roe Whether this was a marriage of love or convenience is not known. Philipp was a woman of high rank in the service of the Queen. In 1367 Chauce was in the service of the King and was granted a life pension as a valet.

In 1370, Chaucer was employed by the King for diplomatic errands and during the next ten years made seven trips abroad. In 1374 he wa appointed controller of the customs in London. That same year he wa given permission to quit the royal residence, and he leased a home in th city of London. Chaucer received other appointments from the King, th most important coming in 1386 when he became a Knight of the Shire

hat same year John of Gaunt, Chaucer's life-long benefactor, left England
r a military foray in Spain. King Richard II promptly stripped Chaucer
f all his customs appointments. When John of Gaunt returned in 1389,
owever, Chaucer was restored to his previous offices.

In the following eleven years Chaucer managed to retain royal favors
nd lived comfortably until his death on October 25, 1400. He was buried
Westminster Abbey. His grave there was the first in what has become
nown as the Poet's Corner.

There is some reliable evidence, therefore, which traces Chaucer's
fe as a civil servant. Very little evidence exists, however, to pinpoint the
fe of Chaucer as a poet.

It is now believed that Chaucer began writing about 1360, and by 1372
e completed most of the translation of *Roman de la Rose* and wrote The
ook of the Duchess and the *Legend of Good Women*. By 1380 he com-
leted *The House of Fame,* the *Paliament of Fowls,* and some of the
tories which later appeared in the *Canterbury Tales.*

By 1385 he translated *Troilus and Criseyde*. About this time he began
e *Canterbury Tales.* (They were never finished, and scholars in later
enturies arranged them in the order thought most likely.) In 1391 he
rote *Treatise on the Astrolabe* and the following year *Envoy to Scogan.*
ust before his death he wrote *Envoy to Bukton* and *To His Empty Purse.*

CHAUCER'S PUBLIC

The public for which Chaucer wrote his tales is important to their
nderstanding. As noted above, Chaucer moved in a high society and
mong the learned members of the Court. His audience, therefore, would
ave been a highly educated, sophisticated, and worldly audience. Chaucer
robably read his tales aloud to this audience. Thus, his hearers would have
ad a knowledge of French, Latin, and English. They would also be familiar
ith the many types of stories, tales, and fabliaus that Chaucer imitated.
herefore, Chaucer could easily utilize various types of classical allusions,
ubtle satire, and irony, all of which would have been fully understood
y his audience.

Chaucer's tales, of course, were not published or read by a general
ublic, but many students of the English language think that they became
o popular that the entire course of the English language was affected by
hem. At the time Chaucer wrote, there were five different accents spoken
n English. These accents varied so much that a person of one section
ould understand another not at all or only with great difficulty.

CHAUCER'S LANGUAGE

The language of Chaucer is Middle English, which, roughly speaking, extends from about 1100 to 1500 A.D. The following explanation may help clarify the linguistic divisions of English for the beginning student of English literature:

OLD ENGLISH *(or Anglo-Saxon)—597 A.D. to 1100 A.D.*
Beowulf, the most famous literary work of the period, is an epic poem in alliterative verse. The author is unknown, but the manuscript (Cotton Vitellius A xv) dates from 1000 A.D.
Example of an Old English half-line from *Beowulf:*
Hwæt we gardena in geardagum—Old English
La. we the spear-Danes in the days of yore—Modern English
(Notice the Germanic quality of the Old English.)
787 A.D.—Danish influence on Old English

MIDDLE ENGLISH *— 1100 A.D. to 1500 A.D.*
Geoffrey Chaucer (*1340-1400 A.D.*) is the acknowledged literary master of the period, and the *Canterbury Tales* is his most famous work.
Example of Chaucer's poetry in Middle English:
At mortal batailles hadde he been fiftene—Middle English
Of mortal battles he had fought fifteen—Modern English
(Notice the French influence on Middle English; also, notice how much closer, linguistically, Middle English is to Modern English than Old English is to Modern English.)

MODERN ENGLISH *— 1500 A.D. to the present*
Some famous English writers of this period—Shakespeare, Milton, Swift, Wordsworth, Dickens, Shaw
Some famous American writers of this period—Poe, Hawthorne, Twain, O'Neill, Faulkner

There is some argument among scholars about the dates for the linguistic periods, particularly regarding the shift from Old English to Middle English. Naturally there was no overnight change from Old to Middle English, but the action which triggered the greatest change was the Norman Conquest of England in 1066 A.D.—thereafter, the English language exhibited a French influence. Typical of the scholarly controversy which centers upon the assignment of an initial date to Middle English is an excellent twentieth-century article by Kemp Malone entitled "When Did Middle English Begin?" (*See Curme Linguistic Studies.*)

TEXTS AND TRANSLATIONS

In many ways, the Middle English of the *Canterbury Tales* is much like

Modern English (unlike the almost foreign language of the Old English in *Beowulf*), and the student of Chaucer should read the Middle English text for full appreciation of Chaucer's poetry. Three excellent books which offer the original text are Vincent F. Hopper's interlinear edition of the *Canterbury Tales* (with selections only, in both Middle and Modern English, line by line), the John Matthews Manly expurgated edition of the *Canterbury Tales* (with helpful commentary and glossary), and the F. N. Robinson complete edition of *The Poetic Works of Chaucer* (including bibliography along with helpful introduction and glossary).

If the student is, for some reason, unable to read the original text of the poem, he should by all means get one of the good modern translations — for example, the poetic translations of J. U. Nicolson or Nevil Coghill. Nevil Coghill points out the variety of meaning which the translator encounters with Chaucerian words. Here is a Middle English line from the General Prologue, for example:

He was a verray parfit gentil knyght

Now according to Coghill, "verray" does not mean "very" but "true," "gentil" means "gentle" but also, and more importantly, of "high breeding" and "good birth." So, to render Chaucer meaningfully and rhythmically into one line, Coghill writes:

He was a true, a perfect gentle-knight.

CHAUCER'S POETRY

Both Manly's and Robinson's explanations of Chaucer's versification are so good that the student or teacher ought to take time to read them. If these texts are not available, however, in the school or local library, the present summary should suffice temporarily.

1. "All of Chaucer's narrative verse, except the 'Monk's Tale,' is written either in rhymed couplets or in stanzas of seven lines."[1]

2. "There is...a difference between Chaucer's English and Present English which is of much importance to the versification. This consists in the fact that a majority of the words in Chaucer's English ended in an unstressed final *e* or *en* or *es*."[2]

3. "The general character of the verse was also affected by the fact that a large number of lines ended in so-called feminine rhymes."[3]

[1] John Matthews Manly, editor, the *Canterbury Tales*, p. 131.
[2] *Ibid.*, p. 123.
[3] *Ibid.*, p. 123.

4. Chaucer used iambic pentameter a great deal (with couplets)—his usage was forerunner of the heroic couplet brought to perfection by Alexander Pope. There were, of course, variations. The heroic couplet is an effective poetic form for satire.

5. The "Tale of Melibeus" and the "Parson's Tale" are the only tales written in prose; the rest of Chaucer's tales are poetic.

A GUIDE TO PRONUNCIATION

Much is lost if Chaucer's poetry is read in translation. It is close enough to modern English so that the student with only a little practice can easily overcome the language barrier. The following brief list of aids will help with the basic differences.

Essentially, the vowels in Chaucer's poetry resemble the modern continental sounds more than they do modern English. The following basic guide is not meant to be a complete pronunciation guide, but functions as a simplified approach to reading the poetry.

1) The *"A"* is always pronounced like the "a" in *father*. In words like "that" or "whan" the "a" sound is shorter than in words like "bathed." See lines 1-3 of the general prologue.

2) The long "i" and "y" are both pronounced like the long "ee" sound found in such modern words as *machine*.

3) The long "e" has the sound of the "a" in such words as *late, hate, mate*, etc. If the "e" is short, give it the modern English pronunciation.

4) The "o" sounds are similar to those of modern English, that is, the majority take the "oh" sound.

5) The "u" is also pronounced approximately the same as in modern English.

6) The following three dipthongs are the most frequent:
A) the "ei," "ey," and "ay" all take the modern "ay" sound found in words like *day, way, pay*.

B) The "au" and "aw" are the "ou" sounds found in *house, mouse,* and *louse*.

C) The "ou" is something in between the "ou" of *you* and the "ew" sound of *few*.

7) The final "e", "es" and "ed"; the final "e" is always pronounced except when the next word begins with a vowel (or "h") and except when he rhythm would be violated in which case it resembles the "uh" and is never stressed.

8) The consonants are essentially the same as in modern English but with more emphasis.

MIDDLE ENGLISH GENRES

According to Baugh's *A Literary History of England,* the *Canterbury Tales* in its extent and variety offers a remarkable anthology of medieval iterature." Baugh then goes on to label the tales according to genre (or iterary type); the following is a simplification of his discussion:

Courtly Romance — Knight's Tale
                 Man of Law's Tale (of Constance)
                 Squire's Tale (fragmentary)

Breton Lay[1] — Franklin's Tale
Fabliaux[2] — Miller's Tale
            Reeve's Tale
            Merchant's Tale
Saint's Legend — Prioress' Tale
Tragedy (through medieval eyes, at least) — the Monk's Tale
Exemplum[3] — Pardoner's Tale
Sermon (or didactic treatise) — Tale of Melibeus
                             Parson's Tale
Beast Fable — the Nun's Priest's Tale

THE GENERAL PROLOGUE

In April the gentle rain, warming sun, and gentle winds, awakened ature from its winter sleep. Then man yearned to travel. In this season n England, from every corner of the land, people made their way to Canterbury to receive the blessings of "the holy blissful martyr" — St. Thomas Becket.

One spring day in Southwark at the Tabard Inn, the narrator (Chaucer) waited the next day when he would commence his journey to Canterbury. That evening a company of twenty-nine persons arrived at the inn, ll of whom were Canterbury pilgrims. Chaucer was admitted to their

A *lay,* in this case, is a short romantic poem, not a song.
A *fabliau* is a short story with a snappy ending.
The *exemplum* was one section of the medieval sermon — the part which set forth examples to illustrate the theme of text of the sermon.

company. Before the pilgrimage began, Chaucer took time to describe his companions.

The Knight

The Knight is the perfect and genteel man who loved truth, freedom, chivalry and honor. He was truly a distinguished man. He had ridden into battle in both Christian and heathen lands and in every instance served his king well. Despite his valorous deeds, the Knight never boasted of his actions nor bored his listeners with his feats.

Commentary

The Knight is the most socially prominent person on the journey, and certain *obeisances* are paid to him throughout the journey. He tells the first story and many pilgrims offer him compliments. One fact that Chaucer's audience would be aware of is that of all the battles the Knight fought in, *none* were in the King's secular wars. They were all religious wars of some nature.

The Squire

The Squire would be a candidate for knighthood. When not in battle, he thinks of himself as quite a lady's man. He takes meticulous care of his curly locks (hair) and is somewhat proud of his appearance. He could also sing lusty songs, compose melodies, write poetry and could ride a horse with distinction.

The Yeoman

The Yeoman was a servant to the Knight and Squire. He dressed all in green and was known as an expert woodsman and an excellent shot with the bow and arrow.

The Prioress

A Prioress named Madame Eglantine was also among the pilgrims. She was a gentle lady whose greatest oath was "by Sainte Loy." She was rather well educated, even though her French was not the accepted Parisian French. She was very coy and delicate. When she ate, she took great care that no morsel fell from her lips and that no stains were on her clothes. She was very courteous and amiable and tried to imitate the manners of the Court. She could not stand pain and would weep to see a mouse caught in a trap. She had three small hounds with her which she treated very gently and tenderly. Her dress was very neat and tidy and she wore a gold brooch with the inscription *"amor vincit omnia."*

Commentary

Chaucer's depiction of the Prioress is filled with gentle and subtle irony. Here is a picture of a lady who happens to be a nun, but she never forgets that she is a lady first. Her oath, "by Sainte Loy," implies that she has chosen the most fashionable and handsome saint who was also famous for his great courtesy. Her emphasis on her appearance and her possessions (including her three dogs) suggest that she secretly longs for a more worldly life. Even the inscription *"amor vincit omnia* (love conquers all) is a phrase that was used both in religion and also in the many courtly romances. And the brooch *is* a piece of lovely jewelry. In general she would be the ideal head of a girl's finishing school in nineteenth century America.

Associates of the Prioress

The Prioress had another nun with her who functioned as her secretary and also three priests.

Commentary

Two of the three priests will relate tales, and one of these tales (The tale of Chaunticleer) will prove to be one of the most popular of all the tales.

The Monk

The Monk was an outrider for his monastery (that is, he was in charge of the outlying property). He owned several horses furnished with the finest saddles and bridles. He loved hunting, fine foods and lots of it; he had several good hunting dogs of which he was very proud. He dressed in fine clothes, some were even trimmed in fur. He was rather fat, very jolly and bald headed. His favorite food was a roasted swan. In general, he favored an outdoor life to that of a closed, indoor existence.

Commentary

Chaucer's art is here demonstrated through his use of irony. While Chaucer never makes a comment about his characters, he arranges and selects his material so that the reader can come to a conclusion about the character. When the monk says that he doesn't approve of the solitary prayerful existence in a monastery, Chaucer pretends to be convinced that the Monk's argument is right. But we see that it is right only because this particular monk tries to justify his non-monastic activities and for this monk, it is the right existence. Everything that the Monk does is a violation of his monastic orders. His love of the worldly goods, food, and pleasures, and his dislike of the quiet monastery contradict his religious vows.

The Friar

The Friar was a wanton and merry man who had helped many girls get married after he got them in trouble. When he heard confessions, he worked under the principle that the penance is best executed by money rather than by prayers. So the person contributing the most money received the quickest and best pardon. The Friar was the type who knew the taverns and inns better than he knew the leper houses and the almshouses. Chaucer says that there was no better man than the Friar when it comes to the practice of his profession. He was always able to get money from people. His name was Hubert.

Commentary

The Friar was a person licensed to hear confessions and to beg for money. This Friar used every vicious and immoral method to extract money from the parishioners, so when Chaucer says there were none so good as Hubert in his profession, he is being ironical. That is, if we judge the Friar by how much money he extorted from people, then he is a great success. But essentially, this Friar is notoriously evil and cunning.

The Merchant

The Merchant was a member of the rich and powerful rising middle class. He is shrewd and knows a good bargain. He talks and looks so solemn and impressive, and transacts his business in such a stately manner that few knew that he was deeply in debt.

The Clerk

The Clerk, who was a student at Oxford, was extremely thin, rode a very thin horse, and his clothes were threadbare because he preferred to buy books rather than clothes and food. He did not talk often, but when he did, it was with great dignity and moral virtue.

Commentary

The Clerk was probably working on his M.A. degree with the idea of attaining some type of ecclesiastical position. Next to the Knight, he is one of the most admired people on the pilgrimage.

The Sergeant of Law

The Sergeant of Law was an able attorney who could recall every word and comma of every judgment, a feat which earned him high distinction and handsome fees. But he makes people think that he is busier and wiser than he really is. There is an implication that he has perhaps used his position to attain wealth without ever actually violating the letter of the law.

The Franklin

The Franklin was a large landowner with a certain amount of wealth, but he was not of noble birth. He spent his money freely, enjoying good food, wine, and company. His house was always open and he was a true epicurean, devoting his energies to fine living and was generally liked by the other pilgrims.

The Haberdasher, The Dyer, The Carpenter, The Weaver, and The Carpet Maker

These were men who belonged to a gild, an organization similiar to a fraternity and labor union. Each was luxuriously dressed in the manner of his calling, and each was impressed with his membership in the gild to which he belonged. The gildsmen had a cook who was one of the best.

The Cook

The Cook was a master of his trade. He knew how to boil, bake, roast, and fry. But Chaucer thinks it a shame that he had a running sore on his hin, because his best dish was a creamed chicken pie whose white sauce might be the same color as the pus from the running sore.

The Shipman

The Shipman was a huge man and somewhat uncouth. He was the master of a vessel and knew all the ports from the Mediterranean to the Baltic. He could read the stars and knew how to fight well. But he did not ride a horse well. He looked like a fish out of water as he sat on his horse.

The Doctor of Physic

There was no one who could speak so well about medicine as this Doctor. He knew astronomy (astrology) and something of nature and could tell what humour was responsible for a sickness. But everyone thought he was in league with the druggist. He could quote all the medical authorities, but knew nothing of the Bible. He had apparently made a lot of money during the plague, but doesn't seem to spend it very readily. Since he prescribes gold for cures, he has a special love for this metal.

The Wife of Bath

The Wife of Bath was somewhat deaf, but was an excellent seamstress and weaver. She made a point of being first at the altar or offering in church. Her kerchiefs must have weighed ten pounds and she wore scarlet red stockings. She has been married five times and has been on pilgrimages to Jerusalem, Rome, Bologna, Galice, and Cologne. She was gap-toothed and rode a horse easily. She enjoyed good fellowship and would readily laugh and joke. Her special talent was her knowledge of all the remedies of love.

The Parson

The Parson was very poor, but was rich in holy thoughts and works. He would rather give his own scarce money to his poor parishioners than to demand tithes from them. His principle was to live the perfect life first, and then to teach it. His life was a perfect example of the true Christian priest, and by his good example, he taught, but first followed it himself.

Commentary

Amid the worldly clerics and the false and superficial religious adherents, the poor Parson stands out as the *ideal* portrait of what a parish priest should be. The same can be said of the following portrait of the plowman. He is the *ideal* Christian man.

The Plowman

The Plowman was a small tenant farmer who lived in perfect peace and charity. He loved God with all his heart. He was always honest with his neighbors and promptly paid his tithes to the church.

The Miller

The Miller was a big brawny man who could outwrestle any man (and even a ram). He was short shouldered, broad and thick set. His red beard

and a wart on his nose from which bristly red hairs protruded made his
look fearful. He played the bagpipes as the pilgrims left the town.

The Manciple

The Manciple was a steward for a law school (or dormitory for lawyers
in London and was in charge of purchasing the food. He was not as learned
as the lawyers, but was so shrewd in buying that he had been able to put
aside a tidy little sum for himself.

The Reeve

The Reeve was the manager of a large estate. He was a skinny man
with a bad temper. His close cut beard and his short haircut accentuate
his thinness and long legs. He was an able, efficient, and shrewd man who
had reaped rich rewards from his master. The serfs, herdsmen, and worker
feared him dreadfully because of his unrelenting perseverance. Like the
Manciple, he had reaped profits for himself by being so shrewd at buying.
He was once a carpenter and rode last among the group.

Commentary

It is not important to the Reeve's characterization that he is a carpenter, but Chaucer is anticipating *The Reeve's Tale* later on. The Miller
will tell a dirty story about a carpenter, and since the Reeve was once a
carpenter, he feels the need for revenge by telling a dirty story about
a miller.

The Summoner

The Summoner (a man paid to summon sinners for a trial before
church court) had a fire-red complexion, pimples and boils, a scaly infec-
tion around the eyebrows, and a moth-eaten beard. Children were afraid
of his looks. He treats his sores as leprosy. To make matters worse, he
loved to eat garlic, onions, leeks, and drink strong wine. He could quote
few lines of Latin which he used to impress people. Chaucer calls him
gentil harlot (genteel fellow) and implies it would be difficult to find a better
fellow, because for a bottle of wine, the Summoner would often turn his
back and let a sinner continue living in sin. He was also well acquainted
with "ladies of questionable reputation."

Commentary

The physical appearance of the Summoner fits his profession well. He
is so ugly and so gruesome looking that a summons from him is in itself a horrible experience. Thus, Chaucer ironically implies that he is
a good fellow. But furthermore, he is a good fellow because sinner
could easily bribe him. The reader should be aware of these subtle
ironic statements which are often made in paradoxical situations.

The Pardoner

The Pardoner was a church official who had authority from Rome to
sell pardons and indulgences to those charged with sins. He had just returned from Rome with a bagful of pardons which he planned to sell to the

gnorant at a great profit to himself. He had a loud, high-pitched voice, yellow, flowing hair, was beardless and furthermore would never have a beard. Chaucer believes he was a "gelding or a mare." But there was no one so good at his profession as was this Pardoner. He knew how to sing and preach so as to frighten everyone into buying his pardons at a great price.

Commentary

The Pardoner seems to be one of the most corrupt of the churchmen. In the prologue to his tale, he confesses to his hypocrisy. And furthermore, Chaucer implies that he is not really a man, that is, that he is either sexually impotent or perverted.

The Host

The Host, whose name is Harry Bailey, was a merry man who liked good company and good stories. He was a large jovial person and was well liked by the pilgrims.

These, then, were the principal members of the party about to leave for Canterbury. That evening the Host of Tabard Inn served the company an excellent dinner after which he suggested that, to make the trip pass more pleasantly, each member of the party should tell two tales on the way to Canterbury. On the return trip each member of the company should tell two more tales. The man who told his story best was to be given a sumptuous dinner by the other members of the party. The Host added that, to keep the journey bright and merry, he would accompany them to Canterbury, and in all things he was to be the judge of what was best for the group. All members of the company agreed to his proposal to act as governor of the journey.

Early the next morning the party departed. Two miles away at St. Thomas-a-Watering, the Host silenced the group and announced that they would draw straws to see in which order the tales would be told. The Knight drew the shortest straw. The Knight agrees to tell the first tale, and here ends the prologue and begins the first tale.

Commentary

If Chaucer had completed his original plans, that of each pilgrim telling two tales going and two coming back, there would have been approximately 120 tales in all.

The Prologue gives an admirable description of the uncomplicated life of England in the Middle Ages. Here are portraits of all levels of English life. In this group Chaucer brings together all of the foibles and virtues of man and the manners and morals of his time with remarkable clarity.

Throughout The Prologue, Chaucer alternately praises or chides the travelers with deftly drawn word portraits which provide insights into the life of his time.

Before Chaucer, there were other groups of tales such as Boccacio' *Decameron,* but never was there such a diversity of people within the same group. It is then a stroke of genius that Chaucer uses the device of the re ligious pilgrimage to bring together such a diverse group.

The shrine of St. Thomas á Becket to which the pilgrims are going was reputed to have great healing qualities. Thus, some of the pilgrims are undoubtedly going for health rather than religious reasons. For example The Wife of Bath was somewhat deaf, The Pardoner was beardless, The Cook had a sore, The Summoner had boils and other skin trouble, The Miller had an awful wart on his nose, The Reeve was choleric, etc.

THE KNIGHT'S TALE

Summary

PART I

Long ago there was once a Duke called Theseus who was the Lord and Governor of Athens. He was also a great soldier who vanquished every foe he met. Among his victims was a realm once known as Scythia, ruled by women called Amazons. Returning home with his amazon wife Hippolyta and her sister, Emelye, Theseus met a group of women dressed in black who were weeping and wailing. They told how each had been a queen or duchess, but had lost their husbands during the siege of Thebes. The cruel tyrant Creon now plans to dishonor the dead bodies.

The Duke, smitten with rage and pity, ordered Queen Hippolyta and her beautiful sister Emelye to return to Athens where they were to dwell in peace. Then, in anger, the Duke and his army marched on Thebes. There on a chosen field of battle, King Creon was slain and the bones of their dead husbands were restored to the mourning ladies.

After the battle was over, two young warriors of Thebes, fearfully wounded, were brought before Theseus. He recognized them as young men of noble birth and was informed they were royal knights named Arcite and Palamon. In appearance, the two knights were very similar, being the sons of two sisters. Theseus ordered that they be returned to Athens as prison ers who could not be ransomed for any sum. They were, he said, to be his prisoners in perpetuity.

Several years passed by, and Arcite and Palamon lay in the prison tower in grief and anguish. On a fair morning in May, however, the beautiful Emelye arose and wandered happily about in her garden, which was ad jacent to the prison tower.

At that moment, Palamon, the sorrowful prisoner, glanced down through the prison bars and saw the beautiful Emelye. He cried out in pain

cite, alarmed, asked him what evil had befallen him. Palamon replied
at the beauty of the young lady had caused him to cry out. Arcite's
riosity was aroused and he peered from the tower window. When he
w the fair Emelye, he cried out that unless he could see her everyday
would die.

When Palamon heard this, he was enraged. After all, he cried to Arcite,
found her first. To counter his argument, Arcite maintains that he *loved*
r first. Thus, even though they are kin and had sworn eternal friendship,
ey decide that in love it is every man for himself. And so the argument
ntinued until their friendship gave way to hostility.

About this time, a famous Duke called Perotheus, a friend of both
eseus and Arcite, arrived in Athens. He implored Duke Theseus to
lease Arcite on the condition that Arcite would leave Athens forever,
d if he happened to return, he would be immediately beheaded.

Arcite then bemoans his fate. Even though he is now in prison, he can
tch a glimpse of his beloved, but in banishment, he will never again see
: fair Emelye. He acknowledges that Palamon is the winner since he can
nain in prison and near to Emelye. But Palamon is equally disturbed
:ause he thinks that Arcite can raise an army in exile, return to Athens
d capture the fair Emelye. Chaucer then asks the reader which position
worse, that of Arcite or Palamon.

PART II

Arcite returned to Thebes where he lived for two years moaning his
rd fate. His lamenting began to change his physical appearance. One
3ht a vision appeared before him and urged him to return to Athens and
: fair Emelye. Acrite arose and looked at himself in the mirror and
alized that his grief had drastically changed his appearance. So he took
: name of Philostrate and returned to Athens where he was employed as a
ge in the house of Emelye. Several years passed, and Philostrate rose to
high and well-to-do position in the Court of Theseus, even becoming a
sted friend of Theseus himself.

Meanwhile, Palamon languished in the prison tower. One night, how-
er, he escaped. He hid in a field the next morning to escape detection.
at same day, by chance, Arcite arrived at the same field. Arcite was so
anged in appearance that Palamon did not recognize him. Arcite, thinking
mself alone, began to recite his entire history aloud. Palamon, hearing
e confession, jumped out of hiding and cursed Arcite as a traitor.

Arcite admitted his identity and challenged Palamon to a duel. The winner was to have Emelye. The next morning Arcite brought armor, food and sword to Palamon. The duel began, and they fought fiercely. At this time, Theseus and his entourage arrived upon the bloody scene.

Palamon explained who they were and why they were fighting. The King, in a rage, condemmed them to death. The ladies of the Court, including Emelye, cried bitterly. Theseus finally agreed to give both of them their freedom on this condition: they should return to Athens in a year, each with one hundred knights. A joust would be held, and the winner would get the hand of Emelye. Arcite and Palamon returned to Thebes.

PART III

During the year, Theseus spent his time building a magnificent stadium in which the fight was to take place. He built an altar to Venus (goddess of love), to Mars (god of war) and to Diana, (goddess of chastity). These altars and the entire stadium were richly decorated with elegant detail which the Knight enjoys describing. At the end of the year, Arcite and Palamon, each at the head of one hundred knights, returned to Athens for the joust. Theseus welcomed them all and entertained them in high fashion with wine, foods, singing, dancing and other forms of entertainment. Again, the Knight enjoys relating all aspects of this magnificent feast.

Before the battle, Palamon goes to the altar of Venus and prays that he be granted possession of the fair Emelye. If he can't have his beloved one, he would rather die by Arcite's spear. Emelye also prays before the altar of Diana. She asks that Arcite and Palamon's love be extinguished and if not, that she be given the one who loves her the most. Diana tells her that it is destined that she marry one of the young knights, but she was not free to tell which one. Finally, Arcite appears and asks Mars for victory in the battle. Mars appears and assures Arcite that he will be victorious.

The three prayers and promises caused some confusion in heaven until Saturn, god of destiny, promised that Palamon would win his love and Arcite would win the battle.

PART IV

The great day for the joust dawned bright and beautiful. The entire populace of Athens swarmed excitedly into the ampitheater. The contestants, on excited steeds, gathered at the ends of the arena facing each other. The great King Theseus arrived and announced that once a warrior was badly wounded he would be removed from the field of battle by the King's marshal, in order to determine the winner without needless loss of life. The milling battle began. Finally, Palamon was badly wounded. Although he resisted the marshals, he was taken from the field.

The victorious Arcite, in his blood-spattered uniform, rode his horse iumphantly around the arena to receive the plaudits of the multitude and ie smiles of the fair Emelye. But all of a sudden a fury arose from the ·ound and so frightened Arcite's horse that the victorous warrior was lunged to the earth. Arcite was badly hurt.

The King returned to his Court, and the populace was happy because all the spectacle of the arena not one man was killed. Even Arcite, it as thought, would survive his injury.

The Duke of Theseus summoned his physicians to attend Arcite. But rcite was dying. Gasping for breath, Arcite protested an eternal love r Emelye and then adds that he knows no person better than Palamon id begs her to think about accepting Palamon in marriage.

Arcite died. His earthly remains were reduced to ashes in a great neral pyre. After a long period of mourning, Theseus summoned Pala-ion to Athens. Then in the presence of Emelye and the court, Theseus de-ared that Jupiter, " 'the King, The Prince and Cause of all and every-ing,' " had decreed that Thebes and Athens should live in peace and that alamon and Emelye should be joined in marriage. They were wed and ved out their lives in "a love unbroken."

ommentary

The Knight tells a tale of ideal love and chivalry. This type of tale ight seem somewhat tedious to the modern reader, but would have been ery popular in Chaucer's day. The reader should notice how well the story s the character of the Knight. He chooses a story filled with knights, ve, honor, chivalry, and adventure. Furthermore, fitting the Knight's iaracter, there are no episodes bordering on the vulgar and no coarse-ess. The love is an ideal love in which there is no hint of sensuality. The ve exists on a high, ideal, platonic plane. The emphasis in the story is oon rules of honor and proper conduct. It is befitting the qualities of a night that he would bring armor to his opponent before they begin to ght. The sense of honor is central to the story and the purity of the love ich knight feels for Emelye tends to ennoble the character.

It is also typical of the Knight that he would love to describe the rich-ess of the banquet and the elaborate decorations of the stadium and the tuals connected with the funeral. This type of richness and magnificence ould appeal to a man of such distinction as the Knight. Furthermore, ie extreme emphasis on form, ritual, and code of behavior are elements f the knighthood.

The modern reader might find it strange that so many elements of *iance* enter into the story. Chaucer himself comments on the role which hance (or Fortune or Destiny) plays during the narrative. The women at the beginning are bemoaning the harshness of Fortune. It is by chance that Emelye walks beneath the prison. Later it is by chance that the Duke Perotheus knew Arcite. Again, it is chance that Arcite is employed by Emelye and later accidentaly meets Palamon. Chance brings Theseus to the same spot where Arcite and Palamon are fighting. And finally, it is the God of Chance or Destiny who determines how the story will be solved. In other words, Chaucer or the Knight seems to be implying that the lives of men are influenced by what seems to be chance, but in the long run and in terms of a total world picture, there is a god who is controlling the seemingly chance occurrences of the world. The universe, then, is not as incoherent and unorderly as might first be expected. There is a *logic* or controlling purpose behind all the acts of the universe even though man might not understand it.

Any reader the least familiar with ancient Greece will be a little surprised to discover that the medieval custom of knights in armor jousting for the hand of a maiden was an attribute of Athenian life. Of course it was not. Yet, we may forgive Chaucer this anachronism. After all, what better way to begin his tales than with the Knight, and a tale of chivalry and romance which a knight would be expected to tell? The Knight does not tell of his own deeds of valor in foreign lands. His tale is about men and women of ages past who lived in dream and fancy. The story could have happended in Greece, of course, but hardly in the trappings of medieval chivalry.

THE MILLER'S TALE: PROLOGUE

Summary
When the Knight had finished his story, everyone said it was a fine story and worthy to be remembered. The Host then calls upon the Monk to tell a tale that will match the Knight's for nobility. But the Miller, who was drunk, shouted that he had a noble tale, and he would match the Knight's tale with his. The Host tried to stop the Miller because of the Miller's drunkenness, but the Miller insisted. He announced that he was going to tell a story about a carpenter, and the Reeve objects. The Miller however, insists. Chaucer then warns the reader that this story might be a bit vulgar, but it is his duty to tell all the stories because a prize is at stake

THE MILLER'S TALE

Summary
Some time ago, the Miller said, there was a rich, old carpenter who lived in Oxford and who took in a lodger named Nicholas. Nicholas was a clerk and was also a student of astrology who, among other things, was able to forecast the likelihood of drought or showers, Nicholas was also a clever young man, neat-appearing, a marvelous harp player and singer, and a lover whose passions were carefully clocked beneath a shy boyish manner and appearance.

Now it happened that the carpenter was married to an eighteen-year-old girl named Alison, and many years younger than the carpenter. Alison was a bright, lively, pretty girl. It was not long before Nicholas fell in love with her. One day he grasped her and cried, "O love-me-all-at-once or I shall die!" At first, Alison made a pretense of objecting, but the young clerk soon overcame her objections. They worked out a plan whereby they would play a trick on her husband, Old John the carpenter. Alison, however, warned Nicholas that John was very jealous.

It happened that sometime later, Alison went to church and there another young clerk saw her, and he was immediately smitten with her beauty as he passed the collection plate. He was the parish clerk and was named Absalon. Chaucer describes this clerk as being very dainty and particular. He is even somewhat effeminate. The final touch to his personality is that he is so dainty that the one thing he could not tolerate was people who expelled gas in public.

That evening with guitar in hand he strolled the streets looking for tarts when he came to the carpenter's abode. Beneath Alison's window he softly sang, "Now dearest lady, if thy pleasure be in thoughts of love, think tenderly of me." The carpenter was awakened but discovered his wife unimpressed with the youth's entreaties.

One day, when the ignorant carpenter had gone to work at a nearby town, Nicholas and Alison agreed that something must be done to get the carpenter out of the house for a night. Nicholas agreed to devise a plan.

And so it happened that Nicholas, gathering plenty of food and ale, locked himself in his room. After several days the carpenter missed the youth's presence. When told Nicholas might be dead in his room, the carpenter and his serving boy went to Nicholas' room and pounded on the door. When there was no answer, they knocked down the door and found the yought lying on his bed, gaping as though dead, at the ceiling. The carpenter aroused the youth who then told of a vision seen in his trance that Oxford was soon to be visited with a rain and flood not unlike the one experienced by Noah. The alarmed carpenter wondered what could be done to escape the flood. Nicholas counseled him to fasten three boat-like tubs to the ceiling of the house, provision each with food and drink enough to last one day after which the flood would subside, and also include an axe with which they could cut the ropes and allow the tubs to float. And finally, the three tubs should be hung some distance apart.

The tub-like boats were hung in place by the stupid carpenter and the evening before the predicted flood all three entered their boats and prayed, When the carpenter fell into troubled sleep, Alison and Nicholas descended the ladder from their boats and sped downstairs, without a word, to bed.

Meanwhile, later that night the young parish clerk Absalon, having heard the carpenter was away from the city, stole beneath Alison's window and begged her for a kiss. "'Go away,'" she cried, "'there's no come-up-and-kiss-me-here for you.'" But he entreated her and Alison, afraid the youth would arouse the neighbors, agreed to give him a kiss. But deciding to play a trick on this bothersome clerk, she extended her rear end out the window which the young clerk kissed most savorously.

When he discovered how Alison had tricked him, young Absalon strode away in anger. He was not completely cured of his lovesickness. He therefore plans revenge. He goes across the street and arouses the blacksmith and borrows a red-hot poker. Returning to the carpenter's house, Absalon knocked at the window again and pleaded for one more kiss. Nicholas decided that Alison's trick was so good that he would now try the same thing, so he presents his rear to be kissed. When Absalon called for Alison to speak to him, Nicholas expelled gas which, as Chaucer says, was like a stroke of thunder. It almost knocked poor dainty Absalon off his feet, but recovering rapidly, Absalon applied the hot poker to Nicholas' arse.

"'Help! Water! Water! Help!'" shouted Nicholas. The carpenter was startled from his sleep, "'Heaven help us,''he thought, "'here comes Nowel's Flood!''" With an axe, he cut the ropes which held his boat to the eaves of the house. Down he crashed. Alison and Nicholas shouted "'Help!'" and "'Murder!'" and the neighbors rushed to the house. Nicholas told them of the carpenter's preparation for a flood. All laughed at this lunacy, and none would help him for they considered him mad. And to conclude it all, the carpenter received a broken arm from the fall.

Commentary

Many who like Chaucer do not like *The Miller's Tale* and choose to skip it. Yet, it is reasonable to assume that stories such as this were rather common in the inns of Chaucer's time. The point here is not that the tale has its bawdy moments, but rather that the reader has enjoyed an expert telling of a practical joke. Is not the point here the stupidity of the jealous carpenter in falling for Nicholas' preposterous flood, rather than the ends for which the trick was devised? With great economy of words, Chaucer's writing here exhibits the deft, concentrated portraiture found in the Prologue to the book.

The reader should also remember that one story is often told in relationship to the story (or Prologue) which has preceded it. Therefore, we should see if *The Miller's Tale* has any relationship with *The Knight's Tale*. We must remember that in the Prologue to the tale, the Miller had promised to tell something which would *match The Knight's Tale*. Consequently, upon reflection, we see that both the Knight's and Miller's tales are involved with a three-way love triangle. In both tales, two men are seeking the love of the same woman. In both tales, the woman remains the more-or-less passive bystander while the men struggle for her. Furthermore, both tales involve destiny or getting-what-comes-to-you. As destiny entered in to solve the dilemma between Palamon and Arcite, so in *The Miller's Tale* there is the sense of every man getting his just desserts. The Carpenter is cuckolded and has a broken arm because of his extreme jealousy. Nicholas has a severly burned rear end. Absalon has been mistreated in another way. One might therefore say that destiny or poetic justice played an important role in both tales. Visions and astrology play a role in both stories. The duel in *The Knight's Tale* is replaced by the window episode in *The Miller's Tale*. The analogies here suggest Chaucer's awareness of the difference between the two narrators. The contrast between the noble Knight and the burly Miller is made more prominent by the type of story each chose to relate. And finally, the type of story the Miller tells is still popular today. Any time a very old man marries a young girl, there will naturally be jealousy and sooner or later, the young wife usually takes on a lover.

THE REEVE'S TALE: PROLOGUE

Summary
After everyone has laughed at the Miller's tale, the Reeve becomes sullen because the tale was unfavorable to a carpenter. The Reeve, whose name is Osewold, promises to repay the Miller with a story. He then tells how he resents the carpenter's advanced age because he is also somewhat advanced in age and can enjoy only a limited amount of things. He points out that in old age, man can only boast or lie or covet. The Host interrupts him and tells him to get on with the tale. Osewold warns the group that his tale will employ the same rough language as was found in *The Miller's Tale*.

Commentary
Once again, the reader should keep in mind the idea that one tale is often told to repay another. Thus since the Reeve is upset over the Miller's Tale, he is now going to tell a tale whereby a miller is ridiculed.

THE REEVE'S TALE

Summary
At Trumpington, not far from Cambridge, there lived a Miller. He was a heavy-set man, a bully, who carried several knives and knew how to use them. No one dared lay a hand on the man for fear of their lives. He was also a thief and always stole corn or meal brought to his mill for grinding. His wife was a portly creature who was the daughter of the town clergyman. She has been raised in a nunnery. The Miller wed her because he was something of a social climber and wanted a refined wife. But Chaucer implies that being the daughter of the town clergyman, she was probably illegitimate. But both of them were proud of their twenty-year old daughter and six-month baby boy.

The Miller levied excessive charges for his work, in addition to stealing what he could. This was particularly true of the corn brought to him for grinding from a large-sized college at Cambridge. One day when the manciple (steward) was too ill to go to the mill to watch the Miller grind his corn, the man sent to the mill was duped and robbed outrageously.

Two students at the college, John and Alan, were enraged when news of the theft reached them. They volunteered to take a sack of corn to the mill for grinding and beat the Miller at his own game. They arrived and announced they would watch the milling. The Miller sensed the students would try to prevent him from stealing some of the grain. He decided therefore that he would take even more than usual so as to prove that the greatest scholar is not always the wisest or cleverest man.

When he had a chance, the Miller slipped out to the students' horse, untied it, and away it ran to the wild horses in the fen. The Miller returned and ground and sacked the corn. The students discovered their horse was missing and chased the spirited animal until dark before catching it. While they were gone, the Miller emptied half the flour from the sack and gave it to his wife.

When John and Alan returned from catching their horse, it was already dark. They asked the Miller to put them up for the night and offered to pay for food and lodging. The Miller sarcastically said to them that his house was small, but that college men could always make things seem to be what they aren't. He challenges them to make his one bedroom into a grand chamber. But he agrees to put them up and sends his daughter for food and drink. Meanwhile, he makes a space in his only bedroom for John and Alan, thus all slept in the same room but in three separate beds: the Miller and his wife in one, John and Alan in another and the daughter in the third. The baby's cradle was at the foot of the Miller's bed.

After drinking for a long time, everyone went to bed and soon the Miller and his family were asleep. But John and Alan lay awake thinking of ways in which to get revenge. Suddenly, Alan gets up and goes over to the daughter's bed. Apparently, they got along just fine. But John stayed in his bed and grumbled about his fate. He then got up and moved the cradle next to his bed. Shortly after that, the Wife had to relieve herself of all the wine she had drunk. Returning to her bed, she felt for the baby's cradle and couldn't find it. She felt in the next bed and discovered the cradle and climbed in bed beside John. He immediately "tumbled" on her, "and on this goode wyf he" layed it on well.

As dawn neared Alan said goodbye to the daughter who suggested that as they left the mill, they look behind the main door and find the half sack of flour her father had stolen. Alan walked over to wake John and, discovering the cradle, assumed he was mixed up and went to the Miller's bed and hopped in. He shook the pillow and told John to wake up. Alan immediately told how he had already had the Miller's daughter three times in this one short night. The Miller rose from his bed in a fury and started cursing. The Miller's wife, thinking she was in bed with the Miller, grabbed a club, and mistaking her husband for one of the clerks, struck him down. Then Alan and John fled the premises.

Commentary

Chaucer has again given us a tale of immorality — not for the sake of immorality but for the sake of a joke. Like *The Miller's Tale,* there is here a rough sort of poetic justice meted out. The Miller had intended to cheat the students, and had ridiculed them when telling them to try to make a hotel out of his small bedroom. During the course of the night, the students had indeed made a type of hotel (house of prostitution) out of his house.

The nature of the two stories (the Miller's and the Reeve's) again testify to the differences in their personality. The Reeve, it will be remembered, is sullen and choleric. His tale is more bitter and somewhat less funny than the Miller's. But on the contrary, the Miller was a boisterous and jolly person, and his tale was the more comic of the two.

THE COOK'S TALE: PROLOGUE

Summary

The Cook, Roger, is laughing over *The Reeve's Tale.* He thought the Miller was well repaid for arguing that his house was too small. He promises to tell a tale that really happened in his town. The Host interrupts and tells him he will have to tell a good one to repay the company for all the stale pies he has sold to them. Then the Host tells that he is only joking. Roger then turns to his tale.

Commentary

Here the Host is playing with words when he tells Roger to tell a good tale to repay the pilgrims for the stale pies. Actually the tale is to repay the earlier narrators.

THE COOK'S TALE

Summary

There was an apprentice cook working in London named Perkin Reveler who was as full of love as he was full of sin. At every wedding he would dance and sing rather than tend the shop. And when he wasn't dancing or singing or drinking, he was gambling. His master finally decided that one rotten apple could spoil the whole barrel. Thus, the master dismissed Perkin. The young man, obeying another proverb, "birds of a feather flock together," joined another young man of the same habits as his. The friend's wife kept a shop, but this shop was just a front to her loose and immoral activities.

Commentary

Most authorities agree that *The Cook's Tale* is only a fragment. Perhaps Chaucer came to feel that three "merry" tales was too much of a dose of humor, thus abandoned it. Nonetheless, we are given a wonderful portrait of a careless young man, even though the ultimate fate he may have suffered for his folly will never be known.

THE MAN OF LAW'S INTRODUCTION

Summary

The Host, noting the rapidly passing day, reminds the company that they must proceed with the tales. Then addressing himself to the Man of Law in what he considers the best of legal language, the Host exhorts the Man of Law to acquit himself by fulfilling his contract to tell a tale. The Man of Law protests that Chaucer has already written about all the good stories of the world and has left nothing else to be told. He also protests that he will not tell his story in rhyme. I am not a poet, he said, but a plain spoken man who will tell a story plainly.

THE MAN OF LAW'S TALE

Summary

PART I

There once dwelt in Syria a company of wise, honest, and prosperous merchants. Their trade in spices, gold, satins, and many other articles was far-flung. It happened that some of these merchants decided to go to Rome to determine if there were opportunities for trade.

During their sojourn in Rome, they heard of Constance, the daughter of the emperor. She was praised for her beauty, her goodness, and her innocence. She was reputed to be the perfect woman, untainted by any of the frivolity of life.

Upon the return of these merchants to Syria, the young Syrian Sultan was, as always, anxious to hear of their good fortune in trading. As the merchants spoke of the wonders they had seen in Rome, they also made special mention of the Lady Constance.

The young Sultan was enraptured with their description of her, and soon his heart was set upon having her as his wife. No one else would do. He took the matter before his council and told them that he must perish if he could not win her hand.

The councilors saw great difficulties. For one thing, the Emperor of a Christian land would not find it convenient to form such an alliance with a nation which worshipped Mahomet. The Sultan cried: " 'Rather than that I lose/ The Lady Constance, I will be baptized.' " Brushing aside objections it was arranged that all of his subjects should become Christians.

All was made ready in Rome for the voyage to Syria. But on the day of departure Lady Constance arose pale and sorrowful for she sorely regretted leaving her homeland and friends.

As plans were being made for the big wedding, the mother of the Sultan was conspiring against Constance and her son. She was angry that her son was making her give up her old religion for the sake of this foreign girl. She called together certain of the councilors and protested that she would rather die than depart from the holy teachings of Mahomet. They all agreed that they would pretend to accept the new religion, but at the climax of the feast, would attack the group and slay them all. The first part ends with the Man of Law attacking the baseness and falseness of the Sultan's mother.

PART II

The Christians arrived in Syria and, amid great pomp, journeyed to the Sultan's palace where he and Lady Constance were overcome with great joy. The wedding ceremony was completed and the dazzling array of dignitaries sat down to a sumptuous feast. At that moment the confederates of the Sultan's mother swept into the banquet hall and all of the Christians including the young Sultan were slain—all, that is, except Lady Constance. She was put aboard a sailing vessel, well provisioned, and cast upon the sea. For days on end her little ship roamed the seas. Finally, one day, the ship beached in the northern isle of Northumberland.

There she was found by the Constable and his wife who took her in and cared for her. This was a pagan land but Constance secretly kept her faith with Jesus Christ. Soon Hermengild, the Constable's wife, became a Christian and then the Constable himself.

Then one night Satan (in the person of a Knight) entered the Constable's home and slit the throat of Hermengild, and when the Constable returned he found the murder weapon in Constance's bed. Forthwith, the Constable took Constance before his king—Alla—who ruled with a wise and powerful hand. The King sentenced her to death but there was such a wailing among the women of the Court, the Knight was asked again if he had killed Hermengild. No, he cried, it was Constance. At that moment he was stricken dead, and a voice was heard to say that the King had unjustly judged a disciple of Christ.

The court was awe-stricken, and soon all were converted to Christianity. All rejoiced at this but Donegild, mother of the King. The King and Constance fell in love and were soon wed. While the King was away at war with the Scots, a beautiful son was born to Constance. But Donegild intercepted the message and wrote a false letter saying the child was terribly disfigured. But the King said if this was God's will, let it be done. Enraged, Donegild intercepted the King's message and wrote a false message that it was the King's will to have the son destroyed. The embittered Constance, aided by the Constable, was taken to a sailing ship and she and her beloved son sailed beyond the horizon.

PART III

King Alla returned from the war, dismayed with the news of his falsi fied messages and grief-stricken at the loss of his son and wife. Donegild was soon discovered responsible, and she was put to death.

In the meantime, the Emperor of Rome heard of the tragic news of the death of the Christians and sent an army to Syria; the culprits were put to death. As the Romans were returning they saw the vessel steered by Constance. Not recognizing her, they took her to Rome where she lived in obscurity, for she had lost her memory and she did not recognize her homeland.

The grief-stricken Alla decided to make a pilgrimage to Rome to seek penance for the foul play which befell his beloved Constance. There, while in the company of a Senator, he chanced to see a child whose face strongly resembled that of Constance. Upon inquiring, he learned of the circum stances. When led to the dwelling place of Constance, Alla told her how his true feeling for their son had been distorted by his mother.

A joyous reunion followed, and then Constance went before the Em peror and acknowledged that she was his daughter. There was great joy in the land. Alla and Constance returned to Northumberland, but within a year the King died. Constance and her son, Maurice, returned to Rome where he later became Emperor.

Commentary

The pilgrims completed their first day's journey to Canterbury, spent the night at Dartford and apparently started late on the second day's jour ney. The Host suddenly confronted the company and told them a fourth of the day had passed. He called upon the Man of the Law to tell his story. The lawyer, all too familiar with contracts, said he would fulfill his obligation.

Chaucer wrote *The Man of the Law's Tale* from an earlier chronicle by Nicholas Trivet, an English scholar and historian who lived in the first half of the fourteenth century. Chaucer considerably condensed Trivet's story.

This story of Constance Chaucer converted from ordinary legend to a great work of art. The author produced his work — we must remember — in the spirit of the Christian Middle Ages when man loved the perfect, the universal, as opposed to the Renaissance which focused its attention on the imperfect individual.

Constance, the beautiful, is the perfect and the universal. We see her in poverty and prosperity, in joy and sorrow, in defeat and in victory. Through out the story Constance is unmoved, unshaken, from the great Christian virtues of humility, faith, hope, and charity. She moves from one improbable situation to another and always, in the end, is miraculously saved. Chaucer does not explain away these events. He accepts them joyously.

THE EPILOGUE OF THE MAN OF LAW'S TALE

Summary

The Host breaks in and congratulates the Man of Law for the excellence of his tale. He then calls upon the Parson to deliver something equally good. But the Parson rebukes the Host for swearing. In turn the Host mildly ridicules the Parson for prudery. Here the Shipman breaks in and maintains that they need a lively story.

Commentary

This fragment is incomplete. It implies that perhaps the Shipman will tell a tale next. But there is much to suggest that Chaucer meant to remove this epilogue from the total picture. Therefore, most scholars prefer the arrangement wherein the so-called Marriage group follows next.

THE WIFE OF BATH'S PROLOGUE

Summary

The Wife of Bath begins her prologue by announcing that she has always followed the rule of experience rather than authority. And since she has had five husbands at the church door, she has had a great amount of experience. She sees nothing wrong with having had five husbands, and cannot understand Jesus' rebuke to the woman at the well who had also had five husbands. She prefers the biblical injunction to "increase and multiply." She reminds the pilgrims of several biblical incidents: Solomon and his many wives, the command that a husband must leave his family and join with his wife, and St. Paul's warning that it is better to marry than to burn. Having shown herself to have a knowledge of the Bible, she asks where it is that virginity is commanded. It is, she admits, *advised* for those who want to live a perfect life, but she admits that she is not perfect. Moreover, she asks, what is the purpose of the sex organs. They were made for both functional purposes and for pleasure. And unlike many cold and bashful women, she was always *willing* to have sex whenever her husband wanted to. The Pardoner interrupts and says that he was thinking of getting married, but having heard the Wife of Bath, he is glad that he is single. She responds that she could tell more, and the Pardoner encourages her to do so.

The Wife then relates stories concerning her five husbands. She recalled that three of them were very old and good and rich. And she will now reveal how she was able to control each one. Her techniques were very simple. She accused her husbands (the first three) of being at fault. She scolded them when they accused her of being extravagant with clothes and jewelry when her only purpose was to please her husband. She railed at her husband when he refused to disclose the worth of his land and the value of his coffers. She derided the husband who considered her as property. She denounced men who refused her the liberty of visiting her friends for women, like men, like freedom. She decried the husband who suspected her chastity was in danger every time she smiled at another gentleman to whom she wished only to be courteous. She denounced the husband who hired spies to determine if she was unfaithful, and indeed, hired her own witnesses to testify to her faithfulness to her marriage bed.

Each time she gained complete mastery over one of her husbands, he would then die. But her fourth husband was different. He kept a mistress and this bothered her because she was in the prime of life and full of passion. Thus, while not being actually unfaithful to her fourth husband, she made him think so. Thus "in his own greece I made him fry." But now he is dead, and when she was burying him, she could hardly keep her eyes of a young clerk named Jankyn whom she had already admired. Thus, at the month's end, she married for a fifth time even though she was twice the clerk's age. And this time she married for love and not riches. But as soon as the honeymoon was over, she was disturbed to find that the clerk spent all of his time reading books, especially books which disparage women. In fact, he collected all the books he could which told unfavorable stories about women and he spent all his time reading from these collections.

One night, he began to read aloud from his collection. He began with the story of Eve and read about all the unfaithful women, murderesses, prostitutes, etc., which he could find. The Wife of Bath could not stand this any more, so she grabbed the book and hit Jankyn so hard that he fell over backwards into the fire. He jumped up and hit her with his fist. She fell to the floor and pretended to be dead. When he kneeled over her, she hit him once more and pretended to die. He was so upset that he promised her anything if she would live. And this is how she gained "sovereignty" over her fifth husband. And from that day on, she was a true and faithful wife for him.

Commentary

The Wife of Bath's Prologue occupies a unique position in that it is longer than the tale. It functions to justify her five marriages and to suggest that the thing women most desire is complete control over their husbands. But in addition to being a defense of her marriages, it is also a confession of her techniques and subtly speaking, a plea for certain reforms for women. She uses two basic arguments: if women remained virgins, there would be no one left to give birth to more virgins, and that the sex organs are to be used for pleasure as well as function. And like the Devil who can quote scripture to prove a point, the Wife of Bath also uses this same technique. Her prologue then refutes the popular theory that women should be submissive, especially in matters of sex. And we should remember that her argument is against the authorities of the church and state and that she is a woman who prefers experience to scholarly arguments.

WORDS BETWEEN THE SUMMONER AND THE FRIAR

Summary

The Friar thinks that this was a rather long preamble for a tale. The Summoner reminds the Friar that he is rather long-winded. The Summoner and the Friar then exchange a few words.

Commentary

This exchange between the Summoner and the Friar anticipate their tales which follow *The Wife of Bath's Tale*.

THE WIFE OF BATH'S TALE

Summary

Once, long ago, a knight was returning to King Arthur's Court when he saw a fair young maiden all alone, and raped her.

The countryside was revolted by the knight's act, and King Arthur was petitioned to bring the knight to justice. The king condemned the knight to death. The queen, however, begged the king to permit her to pass judgment on the knight. When brought before her, the queen informed him he would live or die depending upon how successfully he answered this question: "What is the thing that women most desire?" The knight confessed he did not have a ready answer; so the gracious queen bade him return within one year.

The knight roamed from place to place. Some women said they wanted wealth and treasure. Others said jollity and pleasure. Others said it was to be gratified and flattered. And so it went. At each place he heard a different answer.

He rode toward King Arthur's court in a dejected mood. Suddenly, in a clearing in the wood, he saw twenty-four maidens dancing and singing. But as he approached them they disappeared, as if by magic. There was not a living creature to be seen save an old woman, whose foul looks exceeded anything the knight had ever seen before.

The old woman approached the knight and asked what he was seeking. She reminded him that old women often know quite a bit.

The knight explained his problem. The old woman said she could provide the answer, provided that he would do what she would require for saving his life. The knight agreed, and they journeyed to the Court.

Before the queen the knight said he had the answer to what women desired most, and the queen bade him speak.

The knight responded that women most desire sovereignty over their husbands. None of the women of the Court could deny the validity of this answer.

The knight was acquitted. Then the old crone told the Court she had supplied the knight's answer. In exchange the knight had, upon his honor agreed to honor any request she made of him. She said that she would settle for nothing less than to be his very wife and love. The knight, in agony agreed to wed her.

On their wedding night the knight turned restlessly paying no heed to the foul woman lying next to him in bed. She said, "Is this how knights treat their wives upon the whole?' " Then the knight confessed that her age, ugliness, and low breeding were repulsive to him.

The old hag then gives the knight a long lecture in which she reminds him that true gentility is not a matter of appearances but rather virtue is the true mark of the gentle and noble. And poverty is not to be spurned because Christ Himself was a poor man as were many of the fathers of the church and all saints. All the Christian and even pagan authorities say that poverty can lead a person to salvation. Then she reminds him that her looks can be viewed as an asset. If she were beautiful, there would be many men who would desire her; so as long as she is old and ugly, he can be assured that he has a virtuous wife. She offers him a choice: an old ugly hag such as she but still a loyal, true and humble wife, or a beautiful woman with whom he must take his chances in the covetousness of handsome men who would visit their home because of her and not him.

The knight groaned and said the choice was hers. " 'And have I won the mastery?' " she said. " 'Since I'm to choose and rule as I think fit?' " " 'Certainly, wife,' " the knight answered. " 'Kiss me,' " she said. " '...On my honor you shall find me both...fair and faithful as a wife...Look at me' " she said. The knight turned, and she was indeed now a young and lovely woman. And so, the Wife concluded, they lived blissfully ever after.

Commentary

The Wife of Bath's Prologue and *Tale* is one of Chaucer's most original stories. Yet even here he confesses that he has depended upon "old books." Two are of principal interest, *Roman de la Rose* as elaborated by Jean de Meun, and St. Jerome's statement upholding celibacy *Hieronymous contra Jovinianum*. Yet, Chaucer has created here a work of literary art and good story telling that goes far beyond his source material. The tale is, of course, an *exemplum,* that is, a tale told to prove a point. And the reader should remember that the narrator is an old hag telling a story about an old hag who gained sovereignty over her husband.

In Chaucer's time, the literature was filled with the favorite theme of vilifying the frailty of woman. Chaucer's tale, however, is not a moral diatribe for or against woman. He has created a woman in the person of the Wife of Bath who both exemplifies all that has been charged against women but openly glories in the possession of these qualities. Chaucer goes further. He asks the reader to accept woman's point of view and, perhaps, even feel some sympathy for her.

Chaucer does not make it clear whether he sympathizes with the Wife's opinion of marriage and celibacy, but it is obvious that he did not agree with the prevailing notions of his time about celibacy.

In Chaucer's time, as in a lesser degree today, a second marriage was considered sinful. *The Wife's Prologue* has been described, therefore, as a revolutionary document. This is why Chaucer has the Wife so carefully review the words of God as revealed in scripture. Nowhere, she confesses, can she find a stricture against more than one marriage save the rebuke Jesus gave the woman of Samaria about her five husbands. But this, she confesses, she cannot understand.

There was also, in Chaucer's time, considerable praise for perpetual virginity. The Wife now departs from holy writ and appeals to common sense. If everyone should practice virginity, who is to beget more virgins?

The truly remarkable aspect of *The Wife of Bath's Prologue* however, is not her argument with the mores of her time, but the very wonderful portrait of a human being. She tells the company she married her first three husbands for their money, and each of them died in an effort to satisfy her lust. Her fourth was a reveler who made her jealous and the fifth a young man who tried to lord it over her and when she had mastered him, he ungraciously died. Surely, she moralizes, is this not the tribulation of marriage?

Despite her brash accounting of marriage, one gets the impression she is not sure of herself when she exclaims, "Alas, that every love was sin!" Chaucer has given us a portrait of an immoral woman, a coarse creature to shock her age. But the author does not apologize for her. He leaves the moral arguments in balance. One can only conclude that he believes that unbridled sensuousness is not the key to happiness.

The Wife of Bath's Tale simply underscores the *Prologue*. Here she again pleads for the emancipation of women in the Middle Ages. Many authorities believe that it was not Chaucer's intention to change the filthy hag literally into a beautiful woman. Rather it is a change from a *kind* of ugliness into a *kind* of beauty. Similar tales were widespread in Chaucer's time and he has done little to disguise the fact that he borrowed heavily from them in devising his story.

THE FRIAR'S TALE: PROLOGUE

Summary
     When the Wife of Bath had finished her tale, the Friar wonders if such academic problems shouldn't be left to the authorities. He now offers to tell a tale about a summoner, but the Host admonishes him to let the Summoner alone and tell something else. But the Summoner interrupts and says the Friar can do as he likes and will be repaid for a tale about a summoner by one about a friar.

THE FRIAR'S TALE

Summary
     There was once a summoner for a bishop who had developed his craft to a very high degree. He had a crew of spies, including harlots, who would seek out information on all of the persons living in the parish and such information was to be used against them by the church. Once the derogatory information was in hand, he called upon the miscreants and squeezed exorbitant tribute from them so that their names would not be entered among those doing evil.

     Then one day the Summoner, as he made his rounds blackmailing the rich and poor alike, met a gay young yeoman bearing bows and arrows and wearing a jacket of bright green and a black hat. The yeoman inquired of his calling, and the Summoner replied that he was a bailiff. " 'Well, I'll be damned!' the yeoman said. 'Dear brother,/ You say you are a bailiff? I'm another.' "

     The yeoman said he lived in the far north country and was on his way there. Soon the conversation turned to their vocation of bailiff. " 'From year to year I cover my expenses,' " the yeoman said. " 'I can't say better, speaking truthfully.' " " 'It's just the same with me,' " the Summoner said. " 'I'm ready to take anything.' " They agreed to enter into a partnership.

     The Summoner then suggested a swapping of their names.

     " 'Brother,' " the smiling yeoman replied, "would you have me tell? I am a fiend, my dwelling is in Hell.' "

     The surprised Summoner then asked the fiend how he could appear in various shapes. But the fiend said in effect that the Summoner was too ignorant to understand. Nonetheless the Summoner said he had made a bargain to join forces with the yeoman, even if he was Lucifer himself, and he would honor his word. The bargain was sealed, and they began the journey to the next village.

Somewhat further on, they came upon a farmer whose cart full of hay was stuck in the mud. No matter how he whipped his horses the cart would not move. In exasperation he shouted for the Devil to take all — cart, horse, hay and all. The Summoner urged the fiend to do as he was bid, but the Devil explained that since the curse was not uttered from the heart and in sincerity, he had no power to do so.

Later they went to the home of a rich widow who had consistently refused to pay the Summoner bribes. The Summoner demanded twelve pence, but she again refused. Then he threatened to take her new frying pan. She then became so exasperated at the Summoner's continued threats, she cried "the Devil take you and the frying pan." The Devil asked her if she really meant these words and she said yes, unless the Summoner repented. The Summoner refused. The fiend thereupon dragged the Summoner, body and soul, off to Hell where summoners have very special places. The Friar ends his tale by hoping that summoners can someday repent and become good men.

Commentary

The Wife of Bath began discussing some academic problems. The Friar continues by alluding to the qualities and powers of demons in this world. Since the fiend cannot take the horse, cart and hay, we see that the power of demons is limited.

The height of the irony is that the Summoner thinks the Devil looks enough like him to be his brother. This is the indirect method of commenting on the Summoner's character and occupation.

While reading *The Friar's Tale*, remember that no personal quarrel takes place between the Friar and the Summoner, but rather a quarrel about their professions. The Summoner belongs to the secular clergy which includes parish priests, arch-deacons, and bishops. The Friar, as a member of a mendicant order, belongs to world-wide organizations, holding authority directly from the Pope, and independent of the jurisdiction of the national church. This coexistence often leads to conflict. Thus, the Friar boasts that he is beyond the authority of the Summoner.

Chaucer has relied here on similar stories, but he has given it form and structure which raises it to the level of good literature. The conversation between the fiend and the Summoner is a classic. The shameless Summoner refuses to acknowledge his calling, and even after he learns the yeoman is a fiend, refuses to break the partnership agreement because he finds the fiend such charming if not evil company.

THE SUMMONER'S TALE: PROLOGUE

Summary

After hearing *The Friar's Tale*, the Summoner arose in his stirrups and was so angry that he shook like an aspen leaf. He suggests that the Friar told a well-documented story since Friars and fiends are always good friends. He then recalls the story of the Friar who once had a vision of hell. He had an angel guiding him through hell, but he saw no friars. He then inquired if there were no friars in hell. The angel then asked Satan to lift up his tail, and suddenly millions of friars were seen swarming around Satan's arse-hole. The Friar awoke from his dream, quaking with fear over the very thought of his future home.

THE SUMMONER'S TALE

Summary

In Yorkshire, in a marshy district known as Holderness, there was a Friar who went about praying for his parishioners, and casting a spell over them so that they would contribute money to the Friars. But despite his obvious piety, this priest would go from door to door promising prayers and supplications to the Lord in exchange for anything his parishioners could give him. Following him from door to door was a servant carrying a large sack into which the gifts were poured. Once back to the convent, the priest promptly forgot to make his prayers.

One day he came to the home of Thomas who had been ill abed for many days. The old man reproached the Friar for not having called upon him for a fortnight. The Friar replied that he had spent his entire time praying in Thomas' behalf.

At this moment, the old man's wife entered the house and the Friar greeted her excitedly and kissed her sweetly, chirping like a sparrow. He tells her he came to preach a little to Thomas. She asks him to talk about anger, because Thomas is always so crabbed and unpleasant. But before she goes, she offers the Friar some dinner. The Friar accepted and then suggested that since he lived a life of poverty, he needed little food, but then he suggested a menu sumptuous enough for a king.

The wife adds one more word before she goes. She reminds the Friar that her baby had died very recently and the Friar quickly acknowledged (or pretends) that he knows it because he and the other Friars had seen the child being lofted upward in angelic flight, and they had offered a *Te Deum*, and they had also fasted. He then gives the wife a long sermon or lecture on the virtues of fasting and on the sin of gluttony. He quotes the examples of Moses' forty-day fast, the fast of Aaron and other priests in the temple, and even suggested that Eve was gluttonous.

The Friar then turns to Thomas and embarks upon a long sermon on the necessity of avoiding excessive wealth and the blessings to be received by the "poor in spirit." He recited how those at the convent lived a life of poverty, carefully avoiding excesses of gluttony, wealth, and drink. He ends by telling Thomas how the entire convent prays for him every ight, and Thomas should repay him for his prayers by donating a portion of his gold for an improvement in the convent.

Thomas responds that he has given quite a bit to the friars in the past and he can't see that it has helped very much. The Friar then points out that he has diversified his gifts too much by giving a bushel of oats to one convent, some groats to another, and a penny to this and that Friar. What Thomas should do is concentrate his gifts and give everything to the Friars who then would be the sole authority for Thomas' betterment.

The Friar then returns to his sermon on anger, quoting many authorities connecting the sin of anger with satan and vengeful women. Once Seneca pointed out how a ruler brought about the death of three innocent men because of anger; angry Cambyses, who was also a drunkard, once slew an innocent man, so beware of both anger and drink; and angry Cyrus of Persia once destroyed a river because his horse had drowned in the river. The Friar then tells Thomas to leave off his anger, and instead give of his gold to the Friars. Thomas says that he has given enough, but the Friar insists on something for his cloister. But the sermon on anger and the Friar's insistence only made Thomas angrier.

Thomas then thought a moment and said he had a gift for the Friar if it would be equally shared by all the Friars at the convent. But the Friar would have to swear to share it. He quickly agreed. " 'Reach down...Beneath my buttocks,' " said Thomas, and there " 'you are sure to find/Something I've hidden there.' " Hurriedly the Friar placed his hand on the old man's buttocks. At that moment, the old man let an enormous fart. The enraged priest stomped from the house and made his way to a wealthy lord's house. There, shaking with anger, he told how the old man had offended him. " 'I'll pay him out for it,' " the Friar shouted. " 'I can defame him! I won't be...bidden divide what cannot be divided/ In equal parts.' "

The lord's valet, standing nearby, suggested a way the fart could be equally divided. He suggested that a thirteen-spoke wheel be secured. At the end of each spoke should kneel a friar. Strapped to the hub of the wheel would be the old man. When he passed his gas, the wheel could be turned and thus each Friar could share equally. The lord and lady, all except the Friar, thought the valet's answer all they could desire.

Commentary

The reader should note some of the subtle irony employed in this story. The Friar gives a sermon on fasting and gluttony, but at the same time orders a meal that would be rather gluttonous. He speaks about anger, but in doing so, gets very angry himself. He sermonizes on the value of the "poor in spirit" and poverty, but is openly insistent that money be given to him. And while supposedly chaste, he is somewhat overly familiar with Thomas' wife. Finally from a large view, the story is filled with academic references which seem ironically misplaced in a story which deals with rather vulgar joke.

The coarseness of *The Summoner's Tale* may offend some readers particularly the final part. Yet when considered in the context of the Summoner's vicious story of the wretched hypocrisy of the Friar, the coarse insult suffered is perhaps suitable discipline.

Chaucer has, with outspoken frankness, revealed the Friar for what he is. It is this, and not the plot, which gives the work literary value.

On the face of it, this is a humorous story. Inherent in the tale, however, is a greater moral. Anyone who knows of the sacrifice, nobility poverty, and purity of the early orders of the church makes this tale tragedy rather than a comedy. It was inevitable that the nobility of the early Friars would be turned into the instrument for positive evil at a later time. The Friar in Chaucer's story even parrots the precepts of his pious founder. They become a hollow mockery.

The reader should, perhaps, compare the two sets of tales which were told to *repay* someone else. The Reeve told a tale to repay the Miller. The Summoner tells a tale to repay the Friar. In both cases, the latter tale tends to be the coarser of the two and each time, the last of the two tales has less wit and less subtlety. It seems as though the Reeve and Summoner both rely upon excessive vulgarity in order to repay the previous narrator with viciousness.

THE CLERK'S TALE: PROLOGUE

Summary
After the Summoner concluded his story, the Host turned to the Clerk from Oxford. " 'You haven't said a word since we left the stable,' " the Host said. " 'For goodness' sake cheer up...this is no time for abstruse meditation./ Tell us a lively tale.' " The Clerk bestirred himself and agreed to tell his story, which he said was told to him by a learned gentleman of Italy named Petrarch.

THE CLERK'S TALE

Summary

PART I

In the region of Saluzzo in Italy, there lived a noble and gracious king named Walter. His subjects held him in high esteem. Yet there was one thing that concerned him. Walter enjoyed his freedom to roam the country side and refused to be bound by marriage.

One day a delegation of the lords of the kingdom called upon him and humbly beseeched him to seek a woman whom he would wed. The king was so impressed with their petition that he agreed to marry. Concerned lest he did not mean it, they asked him to set a date and this was done.

The lords even offered to find a suitable bride. To this the king demurred. He would choose the woman and would marry her if they would agree to be subservient to her forever. The lords agreed.

PART II

The day of the wedding arrived and all preparations were completed. The populace was puzzled, for the king had not selected his bride. It happened, however, that nearby there lived the poorest man, named Janicula. He had a beautiful and virtuous daughter named Griselda. The king often saw her as he traveled about and looked upon her form and beauty with a virtuous eye.

Shortly before the wedding was to take place, Walter went to Janicula and asked for permission to marry his daughter. The old man agreed and then Walter sought out Griselda and won her consent. Walter, however, made one condition: he made Griselda promise to always obey his will and to do so cheerfully even if it caused her pain. And furthermore, she is never to balk or complain about any of his commands. Griselda assented to these conditions and they were married.

In marriage, those qualities of patience, virtue, and kindness which Griselda had always possessed began to increase so that her fame spread to all the lands far and wide. People came from great distances simply to behold this paragon of virtue. Shortly afterwards, Griselda bore her husband a daughter. There was great rejoicing because now the people knew that she was not barren and would perhaps bear him a son.

PART III

While the baby was still suckling at her mother's breasts, the king resolved to banish any doubt about his wife's steadfastness to him. He called her to him and told her that one of his courtiers would soon call for the child. He expressed the hope that taking the child from her would in no way change her love for him. She said it would not.

The king's agent arrived and took the child. Griselda did not utter one word which indicated hate for her husband. Time passed, and never in any way did Griselda show loss of love for her husband.

PART IV

Four years passed and then Griselda bore her husband a son, and the people were happy that an heir to the throne had been born. When the son was two years old Walter again decided to test his wife's patience and fidelity. He went to her and told her that she must give up her son. Again she took the news patiently and said that if this was her husband's wish she would abide by his decision in good grace.

When Walter's daughter was twelve years old and the son ten, he decided to put Griselda to one final test. He had a Papal Bull forged declaring Walter free of Griselda and giving him permission to marry another woman. Then he ordered his sister, with whom the children had been placed, to bring his daughter and son home. Plans were then set in motion for another wedding.

PART V

Walter now decided to put Griselda to her greatest test. He called her before him and showed her the counterfeit Papal permission and told her of his intent to marry again. He explained that his subjects thought Griselda of too low a birth and he must take a woman of higher birth. Griselda took the news with a sad heart, but again with great patience and humility, she said that she would abide by her husband's decision and would return to her father's house. She takes nothing with her and explains to Walter that she came naked from her father's house and will return the same, but asks for permission to wear an old smock to cover her nakedness. So she returned to her father who received her with sadness, and there she remained for a short time.

PART VI

Through it all, Griselda went patiently and in good grace about her work helping to prepare the beautiful young girl, whom she did not recognize as her daughter, for the wedding. But Walter could stand his cruelty no longer. He went to Griselda and confessed that the beautiful young girl and the handsome boy were their children and that they had been given loving care in Bologna. He confessed that the cruel tests had been perfectly met by Griselda and that he could find no more patient and steadfast woman. They lived in bliss and when Walter died, his son succeeded to the throne.

The Clerk ends by saying that women should not follow so completely Griselda's example, but everyone should be constant in the face of adversity. And then, addressing the Wife of Bath, he says he will sing a song praising the gentle virtues of Griselda.

Commentary

The reader should remember that this story is told as a result of the Wife of Bath's story about women who desire sovereignty over their husbands. Thus the Clerk tells a story with the opposite view: that of a woman who is completely submissive to her husband.

It is apparent that the Clerk, a student at Oxford, was no grind. The Host's warning against too lofty and pedantic style was not necessary. After the Clerk concluded, the Host declared enthusiastically that the student had told his story in an "honest method, as wholesome as sweet."

The tale was not an original one with Chaucer. As he has the Clerk declare at the outset, Chaucer relied upon Petrarch's *Fable of Obedience and Wifely Faith* which was a considerably shortened translation from Boccaccio's *Decameron*.

What can one possibly conclude from this tale of a virtuous young peasant girl suddenly lifted from poverty and placed among the riches of the palace? Her sweet nobility, however, overcomes both sudden prosperity and also adversity created by her husband.

Is it possible for a woman to possess this overwhelming patience and unquestioning obedience? Perhaps many modern women would consider Griselda a rather ridiculous creature. Chaucer's portrait of this tender maiden may tax one's imagination, yet history is full of actual people and situations which match or surpass the seeming peculiarity of *The Clerk's Tale*.

There is also the question of one's moral duties. Griselda simply did what was common practice at the time she was created by Petrarch: She was a wife, a mother, and a subject of the king. We have little to judge Chaucer's feelings about Griselda.

The character of Walter is another matter. The man is selfish, spoiled, and wantonly cruel. Yet, Chaucer coats this bitter pill by telling us that he is young, handsome, good-natured, and loved by his people. He revels in his eccentric choices of Griselda as his queen and seems to take some pleasure in being cruel to her. It must be said that Walter is thorough. Twelve years of misery for his wife, and seldom do we witness the slightest spark of remorse!

The structure of this story, therefore, grows out of the nature of the two main characters. Walter seems to be as determined to be wanton in his testing of Griselda as Griselda is in being submissive to Walter's perverted demands. Each then possesses a single quality and these are seen pitted against each other.

THE MERCHANT'S TALE: PROLOGUE

Summary
    The Merchant begins by saying he has no such wife as Griselda. He makes it clear that his story will characterize wives of a different sort. The Merchant, who is very old and only recently married, says he got a wife who has put him through hell in only two short months of marriage. His intolerable wife makes his life miserable. The Host begs him to impart a portion of his sorrow.

THE MERCHANT'S TALE

Summary
    In Lombardy, in the town of Pavia, the Merchant began, there lived a prosperous knight named January. When he passed his sixtieth year, the knight decided to abandon a life of wanton lust and marry a beautiful young maiden who lived in the city. His reasons were clear enough. He wished to fulfill God's wish that man and woman should marry. He also wished to have a son to inherit his estates.

The Merchant offers such high praise of marriage and such praise of the role of the wife that it becomes apparent that he is being sarcastic. He then provides many examples of good women — women like Rebecca, Judith, Abigail, Esther, and quotes freely from Seneca, Cato and the Bible. (In actuality, the examples of the good woman are cases where the woman had been the cause of the destruction of a man.)

The matter was discussed with his brother Justinius, and with Placebo. Justinius argued vehemently against marriage, pointing out the faithfulness of women as a major pitfall. Placebo, however, argued the other way and counseled January to make up his own mind, for this was not a matter on which to seek advice.

January finally decided to marry. He looked over the crop of young maidens and chose the beautiful young girl named May. He then called his friends together in order to announce his wedding and ask help in solving a dilemma. He wants to know about the old saying that marriage is heaven on earth. And if he is supposed to have heaven on earth, how can he be sure of choosing the right wife. His friend, Justinius, said that perhaps his wife would be more of a purgatory than a heaven. But January went ahead with the wedding plans. The wedding feast was a sumptuous affair, but it lasted so long that January became impatient for the guests to leave so that he might enjoy his wedding bed. Finally, he was obliged to ask his guests to leave, and when the priest had blessed the marriage bed, he fulfilled his role as husband. The next morning, he sat up and sang like a bird in bed, and his loose skin around his neck also shook like a bird's neck.

It happened that one of January's serving men was a handsome youth named Damian who was smitten with love the moment he first saw the fair May. So remorseful was his unrequited love that he was taken to bed. Upon learning of this, January sent his wife and other women of the Court to Damian's bedside to comfort him. Damian found this an opportunity to pass a note to May in which he professed an undying love for her. Later May responded with a note to Damian acknowledging his desires.

One day January was suddenly stricken with blindness. His heart was sad and as the blindness continued, his evil thoughts of jealousy toward his wife could hardly be contained. He now insisted that May remain by him all the time. He would not let her to go anywhere unless he had hold of her hand. She was nevertheless able to send messages to Damian. By prearrangement, May admitted Damian to the Knight's garden which was kept under lock and key for his personal use. Later that day, May led January into the garden and signalled for Damian to climb up a pear tree.

We leave Damian in the pear tree and visit the gods. Pluto and his wife were discussing the situation involving January and May. Pluto said that he was going to restore January's sight because women are so deceitful, but he will wait till just the right moment to do so. But his wife, Proserpina, said men are so lecherous that she will provide May with a believable excuse.

Later, May led January to a pear tree where Damian was perched. Then she offered to climb up into the pear tree, beneath which they sat, and pluck a ripe pear for his enjoyment. In the tree above, of course, sat Damian. Soon the young couple was locked in amorous bliss. At that moment, January's sight was miraculously restored. He looked up and saw the young couple in an embrace. He bellowed with rage. May, however, was equal to the occasion. His sight was faulty; it was the same thing as awakening from a deep sleep when the eyes are not yet accustomed to the bright light and see strange things dimly. She then jumped down from the tree, and January clasped her in a fond embrace.

Commentary

This is the second tale handling the cuckolding of an old 'sband by a young bride. The first was *The Miller's Tale*. The difference ween the character of the Miller and the Merchant can be seen by comparing the manner in which each tells a similar story.

The choice of names supports the story. January (the old man) marries May (the young woman) after rejecting the advice of Justinius (the just or righteous man) and following the advice of Placebo (the flattering man).

Some have condemned *The Merchant's Tale* as a senseless story of harlotry. There is much more to be said for it. Chaucer has given us one of his finest character sketches in this tale. Old January, now in his dotage, simply bargained for more than he was capable of. Throughout the story, Chaucer's point of view occupies our attention. It is not her faithlessness that concerns us but her very clever intrigue and her supreme audacity of escaping when she is caught. It would have been a simple matter for Chaucer to give the story a tragic ending. The element of tragedy is surely there, yet Chaucer chooses to put his hero into a fool's paradise. The spirit of the story is comedy, not immorality.

THE SQUIRE'S TALE: PROLOGUE

Summary
The Host turns to the Squire and requests another tale of love. The Squire says he will not tell a tale of love but a tale of something else, requesting that he be excused if he says anything amiss.

THE SQUIRE'S TALE

Summary
At Tzarev in the land of Tartary there lived a noble king named Cambuskan. He was excellent in everything and his subjects held him in high esteem. This compassionate monarch begat two sons of his wife Elpheta. They were Algarsyf and Cambalo. Another child, a daughter, was named Canace and no fairer creature ever graced this earth.

At the time of his twentieth anniversary as king, Cambuskan ordered that a lavish celebration be held. In the banquet hall, as the revelry was at its height, there suddenly appeared at the doorway a knight unknown to the people of Tzarev. With humility and grace, this knight named Gawain announced that he had come to the celebration bearing gifts from his sovereign lord, the king of India and Araby.

One gift was a brass horse which could fly faster and farther than any known creature. By pressing a magic lever in the horse's ear, the animal would transform itself from a rigid piece of statuary into a lively yet gentle horse.

The second gift was a mirror which could inform the owner of the innermost thoughts of friends and enemies, and recount the past, and foretell the future.

The third gift was a ring which would enable the wearer to understand the language of any living thing, be it bush or bird; further, the ring enabled the wearer to speak in the language of all these living things.

The fourth gift was a sword which would slay any beast, known or unknown, and cut through even the hardest rock.

The knight was thanked profusely for his gifts and bidden to join the feast. The king, meanwhile, gave the ring to his beautiful daughter. Early the next morning she arose, dressed, slipped on the ring, and entered the palace garden. In a nearby tree sat a female hawk crying piteously. Smitten with compassion, Canace climbed into the tree and, through the power of the ring, inquired of the hawk what had caused her unhappiness. The hawk related the story of how a handsome young male hawk had wooed and won her in marriage and how he tired of her and took up with a beautiful kite. So remorsefull was the jilted female hawk that she left her homeland and wandered aimlessly about the earth. Canace took her to the palace and restored the hawk back to health.

The Squire said he would also tell of how the mirror, horse, and sword profoundly affected the lives of the king and his sons. At this moment, the Franklin breaks in and insists on telling his story.

Commentary
Virtually everything about *The Squire's Tale* resembles countless similar stories found in Oriental literature. Why Chaucer never finished his tale has never been discovered. Scholars have long puzzled over *The Squire's Tale,* perhaps because it is less than half told.

The tale aptly fits the character of the Squire. He had been to strange lands, and had perhaps heard of strange magical events. And similar to *The Knight's Tale, The Squire's Tale* is filled with much elaborate description.

WORDS OF THE FRANKLIN TO THE SQUIRE

Summary
The Franklin interrupts the Squire's tale to compliment him on his eloquence and gentility. He wishes that his own son were more like the Squire or would imitate the Squire's manners and virtues. But the Host is not concerned with gentility, and he instructs the Franklin to tell a tale.

THE FRANKLIN'S TALE: PROLOGUE

Summary
The Franklin interrupts *The Squire's Tale* to compliment him on his eloquence, and he says he will repeat this tale to the pilgrims, but they must forgive him for his rude and plain speech because he never learned rhetoric and never studied the classic orators. And the only colors he can use to enrich his tale are those he has noticed in the meadows.

THE FRANKLIN'S TALE

Summary
   In the land of Brittany, in France, there lived a knight named Arveragus. He was noble, prosperous, and courageous. Yet with all these blessings he wished to take a wife. He found a beautiful maiden named Dorigen. They vowed that they would always respect each other and practice the strictest forbearance towards each other's words and actions. Thus solemnly pledged, they were wed.

   Soon after the marriage, Arveragus had to go to a distant land for two years to replenish his wealth. While he was absent, Dorigen was so unhappy, forlorn, and grief stricken with her husband's absence that she sat and mourned and refused to join her neighbors in revelry.

   Nearby to Dorigen's Castle was the rocky coast of France. In her grief, she often sat on the shore, observed the rocks, and meditated on the reason of existence. The sight of the grisly bare rocks made her apprehensive for her husband's safety because many men had lost their lives upon these dreadful rocks. She even wonders why God allowed so many men to be killed on these rocks, and wishes they would disappear into hell.

   One day in May, however, she attended a gay picnic. Also present was Aurelius who had been secretly and madly in love with Dorigen. He mustered enough courage to approach and tell her of his love for her. She repudiated his advances. He became so despondent she believed she must do something to raise him from his depths of despair. She said, half-jokingly, that she'd agree to his embraces if he would remove all the rocks from the coast of Brittany. But this was impossible, he cried. Aurelius returned home where he prayed to Apollo to send a flood which would cover the rocks so that he might then hold Dorigen to her promise. He went into a spell of complete despondency and was cared for by his brother.

   Meanwhile Arveragus returned home and was joyfully reunited with Dorigen. But to return to Aurelius; for two years he lay sick because of his unrequited love for Dorigen. During this time, his brother cared for him and was told of his love. Then the brother thought of a way to solve the dilemma. He knew of a student in southern France who claimed to have deciphered the secret codes of magic found in rare books. Aurelius went to him and promised payment of 1,000 pounds if his magic would clear the coast of rocks. The student agreed and the deed was performed. Aurelius then asked Dorigen to keep her promise. When Arveragus returned, he found his wife prostrate with grief. She told him the story of her bargain and he said she must keep her promise, although it would grieve him deeply. Dorigen presented herself to Aurelius. When he learned of the nobility and sacrifice of Arveragus, he could not force himself to possess Dorigen and sent the relieved woman back to her husband. Aurelius gathered all of his gold together and found he could only pay half of his fee owed the student. The student, when told that Dorigen was relieved of her part of the bargain, acquired a noble demeanor and forgave Aurelius of his debt. The Franklin concluded, "Which seemed the finest gentleman to you?"

Commentary

The Franklin is somewhat subservient in the way he insists upon paying compliments to the Squire and in the way he sides with the Clerk in emphasizing the need of patience in marriage. In fact this tale is connected with many that precede it. The Knight's and Miller's Tales involve a three-way love affair. The Franklin is also striving for something in between the complete sovereignty advocated by the Wife of Bath and the patience suggested by the Clerk. The Franklin's couple base their marriage on mutual trust and faith in each other.

The chief virtue of *The Franklin's Tale* is the noble spirit which pervades it. Here we have the beautiful Dorigen who refuses to be unfaithful while her husband is away; the duty to keep a promise even though it may be spoken in jest. Indeed, so powerful are the words of good here that the lover and the poor student are obliged to accept a degree of nobility. Supporting all this is Chaucer's main theme that love and force are antithetical, and patience and forbearance are the essence of love. Chaucer is not one, however, to let a story become overly sentimental, and throughout the tale sly humor makes its appearance.

The Franklin's question—which of the three seemed to be the finest gentleman—probably cannot be answered. This literary device, however, surely provokes a picture of heated debate between the members of the company. Perhaps many of us will agree that Arveragus erred when he demanded that his wife make a sacrifice for a pledge made in jest. Nonetheless, his noble deed begets nobility from the other two, demonstrating that is is possible for good to overcome evil.

THE PHYSICIAN'S TALE

Summary

There was once a knight named Virginius who was rich, kindly, and honorable. The knight had only one child, a beautiful fourteen-year old daughter. Her beauty was beyond compare, and she was endowed with all the other noble virtues: patience, kindness, humility, abstinence and temperance. The Physician then departs from his story and addresses all people who are involved with bringing up children, telling them that they must set the example for the child.

Returning to his story, the Physician said the girl and her mother went to the town one morning. On the street a judge named Appius saw her. He was taken by her beauty and was determined to have her. After pondering on a scheme, he sent for the town's worst blackguard, called Claudius and paid him well to take part in the plan.

Claudius then accused the noble knight of having stolen a servant girl from his house many years ago and has kept her all these years pretending that she is his daughter. Before the knight had a chance to call witnesses, Appius the judge ruled that the child must be brought to him immediately as a ward of the court.

Virginius returned home and called his daughter into his presence. She must, he said, accept death, or shame at the hands of Claudius. Since the knight could never accept the shame, he withdrew his sword and cut off his daughter's head. Holding it by the hair, he went to the judge and handed it to him. The judge ordered the knight hung for murder. At that moment a throng of citizens, aroused by the judge's treachery, threw the judge into prison. Claudius was to be hung but the knight pleaded for his life and suggested only exile, which was done. "Here," said the Physician, "one can see how sin is paid its wages."

Commentary

The Physician's Tale begins, "Livy has handed down a tale to us..." There is no doubt that Titus Livius' history is the source of Chaucer's tale, but there is a substantial difference between them. Indeed, students of Chaucer now believe that Chaucer never consulted Livy at all but borrowed this story from Jean de Meun's *Roman de la Rose*. Chaucer's tale puts the emphasis on the loveliness and chastity of the girl, whereas the French version places the most emphasis on the unjust judge and the punishment meted out to him.

Chaucer's story, however, is made much more interesting by added description and the introduction of dialogue, particularly between Virginius and his daughter.

THE PARDONER'S TALE

WORDS OF THE HOST TO THE PHYSICIAN AND THE PARDONER

Summary

The Host was terribly upset by *The Physician's Tale*. He called the judge a low blackguard and treacherous man. The Host thinks that the pilgrims need a merry tale to follow and turns to the Pardoner who agrees to tell a merry tale. The more genteel members of the company fear that the Pardoner will tell a ribald story and ask for something with a moral. The Pardoner asks for something to drink, and he will tell a moral tale.

THE PARDONER'S PROLOGUE

Summary

The Pardoner explains to the pilgrims his methods used in preaching. He always takes as his text *Radix malorum est* (Love of money is the root of all evil). His technique is as follows: first, he shows all of his official documents, then he uses some latin; following that he shows his relics which include a sheep bone for good luck in preventing diseases in animals and will bring a man wealth and cure jealousy; a mitten which will bring more money when the Pardoner receives his money for the relic. Addressing himself to the audience, he announces that he can do nothing for the really bad sinners, but if all the good people will come forward, he will sell them relics which will absolve them from sins. In this way he had won a hundred marks in a year. Next, he stands in the pulpit and preaches very rapidly over the sin of avarice so as to intimidate the members into donating money to him. He acknowledges that many sermons are the result of selfish and evil intentions, and he even admits that he spits out venom under the guise of holiness; and even though he is guilty of the same sins he is preaching against, he can still make other people repent.

The Pardoner then admits that he likes money, rich food, and fine living. And even if he is not a moral man, he can tell a good moral tale.

Commentary

The Pardoner's Prologue is in the form of a confession. Even though he is essentially a hypocrite in his profession, he is at least being honest here as he makes his confession.

Notice that he takes as his text that "Love of money is the root of all evil," but with each relic, he emphasizes how it will bring the purchaser more money. And in emphasizing this, he sells more, and gains more money for himself. Thus there is the double irony in his text, since his love for money is the root of his evil, and his sales depend upon the purchaser's love for money. Furthermore, his technique of relying upon basic psychology by selling only to the good people brings him more money. His sermon on avarice is given because the Pardoner is filled with avarice, and this sermon fills his purse with money.

THE PARDONER'S TALE

Summary

In Flanders, three young men sat in an inn after drinking, gambling, and swearing all night long. The Pardoner now stops his tale and gives a rather long sermon directed against drinking, gambling, and swearing, and gluttony. He suggests that gluttony was the cause of Lot's incest, it caused Herod to have John the Baptist beheaded, and it caused Eve to eat the fruit. He quotes St. Paul and elaborates more on the sin of eating and drinking to excess. He then attacks cooks who contribute to gluttony by preparing dishes too succulently. He turns to wine and drunkenness and quotes authorities and examples to affirm the evil of drinking. This leads him into saying how evil gambling is since it leads to lying, swearing and waste of property. He cites again the history of gambling. He closes his sermon with a long diatribe against swearing.

He returns to these three rioters "of whiche I telle" who were drinking when they heard bells sounding which signified that a coffin was passing the inn. The young men asked the servant to go and find out who had died. The lad told them it was not necessary since he already knew. The dead men was a friend of theirs who was stabbed in the back the night before by some sneaky thief called Death—the same thief who took so many lives in the neighboring town recently. The young rioters thought that Death might still be in the next town, and they decided to seek him out and slay him. On the way, they met an extremely old man dressed rather poorly. The rioters comment on his advanced age. He explains that he must wander the earth until he can find someone who will be willing to exchange youth for age. He says that not even Death will take his life. Hearing him speak of Death, the three young rioters ask the old man if he knows where they can find Death. He told the three men that he had last seen Death under a tree at the end of the lane. The rioters rush to the tree and find instead eight bushels of gold. They decide to keep the gold for themselves, but are afraid to move it in the daytime. They decide to wait for the night, and they draw straws to see which one will go into town to get food and wine to hold them over. The youngest of the three drew the shortest straw and started for town. As soon as he had left, the two decided to kill the youngest and split the money between them. But the youngest decided that he wanted all of the money. He goes to the druggist and buys poison that will kill rats quickly. He buys three bottles of wine and pours the poison into two of them. When he approaches the tree, the two immediately stab him and then they sit down and drink all of the wine. Thus ended these homicides.

The Pardoner now decries against sin and reminds the pilgrims that he has pardons that they can buy. He invites them to buy from him and he will immediately record their names as purchasers. He suggests that the Host should begin since the Host is the most sinful. But in turn, the Host attacks the Pardoner, intimating that the Pardoner is not a full man. The Pardoner became so angry he could not speak. The Knight restored peace and they rode forth on their way.

Commentary
The Pardoner is one of the most complex figures in the entire pilgrimage. He is certainly an intellectual figure; his references and knowledge and use of psychology attest to his intellect. But in making his confessions to the pilgrims about his hypocrisy, he seems to be saying that he

wished he could be more sincere in his ways, except that he does love money and power too much.

His tale is told to illustrate his preaching methods. It is often considered one of the finest examples of the short story. Its brevity and use of dialogue and its quick denouement fufill the standards for a good short story.

There has been much argument as to the meaning of the old man. Perhaps he is death itself, or perhaps a mystic figure like the "Wandering Jew." But his function in the story is clear. He is the instrument by which the three rioters find Death. And for the Pardoner, a conscious practitioner of hyprocrisy, this old man is a splendid example of hyprocrisy in the way he deceived the three rioters.

Note that at the end, the host implies that the Pardoner is not a full man. We know from *The General Prologue* that he has no beard, and now it is implied that he is perhaps impotent or perverted. Perhaps it is this condition which causes the Pardoner to be so cynical, and yet there are suggestions that he would like to be different.

The popularity of this tale is easy to understand. It is a tragic story, or at least an ironic tragedy. It is the Pardoner's own lesson: the love of money is the root of all evil, and those who covet money covet death and find it.

The Pardoner's Tale, however, is Chaucer's adaptation of a popular fable thought to have its origins in the Orient. It is not possible to determine the exact source of Chaucer's story. Here again, however, the artistry of Chaucer is evident. No known fable bearing this plot employs the dark background of the Plague or the sinister figure which the three drunken men meet in their search for Death.

THE SHIPMAN'S TALE

Summary
There once was a merchant in St. Denys, the Shipman began, who was rich and had an uncommonly beautiful wife. They lived in a splendid house which, more often than not, was filled with guests.

Among these guests was a handsome young monk about thirty years old. The young monk was on the best of terms with the kind hearted merchant. Indeed, to avail himself of the merchant's hospitality the young monk stated that they were cousins, or very nearly related, since both were born in the same town. So happy was the merchant about this relationship he vowed he would always regard the monk as a brother.

It happened that the merchant, as was the custom in those days, planned to go to Brussels to purchase wares. He invited the young monk to his home for a few days before he left. The monk gladly accepted.

On the third day of the monk's visit the merchant went to his counting room to total up his debts and money to see where he stood financially before he left for Brussels. While the merchant was thus engaged, the monk was in the garden. Soon the merchant's wife entered the garden. The monk remarked that she looked quite pale and suggested wryly that perhaps her husband had kept her awake all night at play. " 'No, cousin mine,' " the merchant's wife protested, " 'things aren't like that with me.' " She then said she could kill herself because things had gone so badly with her.

The monk then said, " 'God forbid...Unfold your grief...' .'" She agreed to tell him her problem of marital neglect if both swore themselves to secrecy. They took a solemn vow, and she told the story, and apologized for berating the monk's cousin. " 'Cousin indeed!' " the monk cried, " 'He's no more cousin to me/ Than is this leaf, here, hanging on the tree.' "

Finally, the merchant's wife begged the monk to loan her one hundred francs to buy some things her frugal husband had denied her. The monk agreed to bring her the money as soon as the merchant left for Brussels. Then he drew the wife to him and kissed her madly.

After dinner that night, the monk drew the merchant aside and begged him for a loan of one hundred francs to purchase some cattle. The merchant gladly gave him the money.

The next day the merchant left for Brussels. Soon after, the monk arrived at the merchant's home and, as agreed, in exchange for the money, the wife agreed to spend the night in bed with the monk.

Some time later the merchant made another business trip and on his way stopped by the monk's abbey to pay a social call, but not to collect the loan. The monk, however, said he had paid the money to the merchant's wife only a day or two after it had been loaned.

When the merchant returned home, he chided his wife for not having told him the loan had been repaid. Then she explained that she had used the money to buy fine clothes. The merchant saw that there was no point in scolding her further and concluded, " '...Well, I forgave you what you spent,/But don't be so extravagant again.' "

Commentary

This tale fits the personality of the Shipman. A thief and a pirate, he tells a grossly immoral story. The monk not only betrayed his vows as a man of God, but also had a deliberate disregard for common decency toward a man who had opened his home to him. Indeed, he falsely cultivated the merchant's friendship by professing that they were in some way related. The monk then went further by betraying the merchant's wife. Finally, the monk left her in an embarrassing situation about the loan.

The laugh is on the merchant and his wife. The moral of the story is, perhaps, that adultery can be very amusing and profitable, provided that it is not found out. Chaucer's tale has a fine sense of narrative and the characters are well-designed but yet there remains the rather distasteful portrait of lust and treachery.

This story is presumed to have been originally told as a French fable. There is a question, however, about why Chaucer assigned this tale to the Shipman. At the beginning of the tale, the narrator says our husbands want us to be hardy, wise and good in bed. The use of the pronoun suggests that Chaucer intended to assign this story to one of the female members of the party, and probably by the nature of the tale, intended it for the Wife of Bath. When he changed his mind, Chaucer apparently forgot to eliminate this inconsistency.

THE PRIORESS' TALE: PROLOGUE

Summary
The Prioress begins by addressing the Virgin Mary and extolling the praises of Mary. The prologue is thus a hymn of praise, in which the virtues of the Virgin are praised.

THE PRIORESS' TALE

Summary
In a Christian town in Asia, there was one quarter of the town where Jews lived. They were kept by the lord of the town for usurious purposes.

At the far end of the street through the ghetto stood a school for young Christian children. The children were free to walk through the street to and from school.

One of the pupils was a mere child who had not learned to read and was only beginning to recognize the Latin of his prayers. At school he heard the older children singing *O Alma Redemptoris*. Day after day he drew near as they sang and listened carefully. Soon he had memorized the first verse even though he had no notion of what the Latin meant. One day he begged another lad to tell him what the song meant and the older lad said:

> "...This song, I have herd seye,
> Was maked of our blisful Lady free,
> Hire to salue, and eek hire for to preye..."

Thus when the child learned that the song was in praise of the Virgin Mary, he was delighted and decided to learn the entire song so that on Christmas day he would pay reverence to Christ's mother.

So every day the child would go along the Jewish street singing the song boldly and clearly. At about this time the Serpent Satan whispered to the Jews that this singing boy was a disgrace to them and the singing was being done to spite the Jewish Holy Laws.

The Jews then began conspiring. A murderer was hired and one day he grasped the child, slit his throat, and tossed his body in a cesspool.

The child's mother, a widow, waited all that night. When the sun rose, she went to the school where she got the news her son was last seen in the street of the Jews. She made inquiry of the Jews from house to house, and all said they knew nothing of the child. Then Jesus put in her thoughts the direction to the alley where he had been murdered and the pit where her boy was cast.

As the widow neared the place, the child's voice broke forth singing *O Alma*. The Christian people gathered around in astonishment. The Provost of the city was called, and upon seeing the child, bade all Jews be fettered and confined. They were later drawn by wild horses and then hanged.

The child was taken to a neighboring abbey. As the burial mass drew near, the child continued to sing *O Alma* loud and clear. He then told the abbots that Christ had commanded him to sing until his time for burial and that, at the same moment, the Virgin Mary laid a grain upon his tongue.

" 'And...I must sing,' " the child said, " 'For love of her,.../ Till from my tongue you take away the grain.' " The monk took away the grain, and the child "gave up the ghost...peacefully." Later a tomb of marble was erected as a memorial to the young boy.

Commentary

The Prioress' Prologue is aptly fitted to her character and position. She is a nun whose order relies heavily upon the patronage of the Virgin Mary. Furthermore, her hymn to the Virgin Mary acts as a preview to the tale which concerns the same type of hymn of praise sung for the Virgin.

To understand *The Prioress' Tale,* one must first understand the background for tales such as these. In medieval England, the Christian hatred for the Jews took the form of a religious passion. This passion was periodically renewed by stories such as this one and passed along as true.

The first story of this sort was written by Socrates in the fifth century. The story was "localized" in 1144 when St. William of Norwich was supposed to have been murdered by Jews. The number of these martyrdoms has never been accurately accounted for, but one authority in 1745 recounted fifty-two. The belief persists in some parts of Europe today.

A legend so widespread as this could not fail to appear in the literature of Chaucer's time, although the particular source of his story has never been discovered.

In this tale, as in so many of Chaucer's, the author lays most of the emphasis on the human aspects of the tale rather than the supernatural. Chaucer, of course, has not slighted the glories of the Virgin Mary nor the wickedness of the Jews. But his chief interest centers on the child and his mother.

SIR TOPAS: PROLOGUE

Summary
    The Prioress' Tale of the miracle of the child naturally sobered the pilgrims. But soon the Host told jokes to liven the group and then turned to Chaucer. He asks "what kind of man are you since you are always looking at the ground." The Host then comments on Chaucer's physical appearance and tells him to come forth with a tale. Chaucer explains that he knows only one story; it is in rhyme and he heard it a long time ago.

CHAUCER'S TALE OF SIR TOPAS

Summary
    The Prioress' tale of the miracle of the child naturally sobered the pilgrims. But soon the Host told jokes to liven the group and then turned to Chaucer. " 'Who might this fellow be?" He inquired, and then suggested that Chaucer tell his story.

Far across the sea, in Flanders, there lived a young knight by the name of Sir Topas. His father was a titled nobleman who possessed much wealth.

Sir Topas was a handsome man. He was a great hunter, an accomplished archer, and a skilled wrestler. Every maiden in the land spent restless nights pining for his love. But Sir Topas took little interest in these maidens.

So, one day, he rode away to the forest and after an exhausting ride, he paused at nightfall beside a watering place. When he fell asleep he dreamed that an Elf Queen had slept beneath his cloak. When he awoke he was determined that he would ride to the ends of the earth in search of an Elf Queen. Nothing would requite his love.

He rode on. Soon he met a three-headed giant who bade him depart this part of the forest, for it was the kingdom of the Elf Queen. The Giant threatened death should Sir Topas fail to leave. The knight accepted the challenge and then rode away to his home to secure his armor and prepare for the great battle with the giant.

58

At his father's castle he feasted elegantly and prepared for the battle with the finest armor and weapons.

HERE THE HOST STINTETH CHAUCER OF HIS TALE OF TOPAS

Summary
The Host interrupts Chaucer crying "For God's sake, no more of this." And he added, "I am exhausted by these illiterate rhymes." He then asks Chaucer to leave off the rhymes and tell something in prose. Chaucer agrees to tell a *little* thing in prose, but warns that he might repeat some of the proverbs that the pilgrims have heard before.

Commentary
It is, of course, ironic that Chaucer says to the Host that these are the best rhymes that he can do. Each stanza is filled with traditional clichés and absurd speech. Chaucer was making fun of himself, ridiculing this type of literature, and belittling the people who read this type of poetry. And most ironic of all is that Chaucer assigns this silly tale to himself.

Furthermore, when the Host interrupts Chaucer, he pretends to be a little offended saying that these are his best rhymes. And then Chaucer promises a *little* thing in prose with a few familiar proverbs, but he proceeds to write a long, dull tale that rambles on forever and is filled with many proverbs.

The Tale of Sir Topas has long puzzled scholars. At the time Chaucer wrote it, there were already in existence scores of tales of handsome knights in search of adventure and fair maidens. All of them were naively simple, long-winded, larded with minute descriptions, and plotted with improbability.

CHAUCER'S TALE OF MELIBEE

Summary
The principal character in the tedious debate is Dame Prudence, the wife of Melibee. The principal subject is whether we should avenge a violent injury by further violence. It so happened that when Melibee and his wife were away three burglars entered their home and seriously injured their daughter Sophia. The question was: Should they take revenge upon the burglars?

In the course of the argument a variety of subjects arise and are dealt with in a learned manner by doctors, lawyers, clerics and many others. These subjects included the importance of not making God an enemy, whether women are to be trusted, and whether private revenge is dangerous, or morally justifiable, or expedient.

Finally, the three burglars are found and brought before Dame Prudence who astonished and delighted the ruffians by her suggestion of a peaceful settlement. Her husband, Melibee, decided to let them off with a fine, but Dame Prudence vetoed this. Melibee then forgave the burglars, rebuked them, and extolled his own magnanimity. What happened to Sophia was never learned.

Commentary

The Tale of Melibee is, as one authority describes it, a prime example of a literary vice of the Middle Ages—an essay abounding in dull commonplaceness, forced allegory, and spiritless and interminable moralizing. Some think this tale is a mischievous companion to Chaucer's Tale of Sir Topas. At any rate, the tale was not Chaucer's own but a translation of a French tale, Le Livre de Melibee et de Dame Prudence, which in turn had been translated from the Latin work, Liber Consolationis et Consilli by Albertano.

THE MONK'S TALE: PROLOGUE

Summary

The Host, true to his middle-class upbringing in medieval England, was delighted with the marvelous tale of Dame Prudence, the benign, gentle, and understanding woman. Crowed he: "'As I'm an honest man...I'd rather have had my wife hear this tale....'" His wife, he explained, drove him continually to acts of dishonesty and violence.

Then the Host turned to the Monk and demanded a story which he confidently expects to be a merry tale, But he is disappointed, for the Monk began a series of tales in which tragedy was the theme. Some of the stories he warned might be familiar to his hearers and some might not.

THE MONK'S TALE

Summary

After reciting briefly the fall of Adam and Lucifer, the Monk told the story of Samson whose great feats of strength made him ruler of Israel. But tragedy befell him when he married Delilah and told her one night that his strength was in his hair. To his enemies Delilah sold the secret. They clipped away his hair, put out his eyes, and threw him in a cave where he was the subject of jeers. One day he was asked to show his feats of strength and, his power restored, he destroyed the temple of his enemies and its 3,000 inhabitants. The monk moralized that men should not tell their wives secrets that should remain secret.

Next the Monk related the story of Hercules and how his great feats of strength and bravery led him into all the regions of the earth where he slew an infinite variety of monsters. Hercules fell in love with the beautiful

Deianira and soon she fashioned him a gay shirt, But its fabric was poisoned and when he donned it his life ebbed. Disdaining death by poison, Hercules threw himself into a fire. Let all successful men, the Monk moralized, beware how Fortune elects to plot their overthrow.

The Monk continued with the stories of *Nebuchadnezzar* who was turned into an animal until he repented his idolatrous sins, and of *Balthasar* who refused to abandon the ways of the wicked, despite God's warning, and ultimately lost his kingdom.

The Monk's seventh story was of *Zenobia,* a Persian woman who was not only beautiful but of great strength and courage. She feared neither man nor beast. One day she met and fell in love with Prince Idenathus, also a great warrior. They were wed and she bore him two sons. Zenobia and her husband swept all foes before them and ruled a vast region as far away as the Orient. The Prince died but Zenobia and her sons continued to rule and showed their captive nations no mercy. Then one year Aurelius, the great Roman emperor, invaded Zenobia's kingdom, took her and her sons captive, and in Rome they were jeered and gaped at.

The Monk then said that the mighty must always be on guard against treachery. He related briefly stories to prove his point. *King Peter of Spain* was betrayed and slain by his own brother. *King Peter of Cyprus* was slain by his own companions. *Bernabo of Lombardy* was killed in prison at the instigation of his nephew. *Count Ugolino of Pisa* was imprisoned with his three children and left to starve. After some time, the children began to cry out for bread. Then the youngest died. The count began to gnaw his own arm and one of the children offered his own flesh. Finally the other children starved and later the Count also died from starvation. Thus many of the mighty, after reaching the height of power, are betrayed and brought low.

Men who rise to power and fame are also dangerous to themselves. *Nero* rose to great fame. He loved all the fine and delicate things in the world. To satisfy his imagination, he had Rome burned, he killed people simply to hear the sounds of weeping and he even killed his mother so as to cut open her womb and observe his place of birth. But when his time was up, he could find no person who would shelter him or even kill him. He finally had to kill himself.

Holofernes was once so powerful that he made the entire world give up worship of individual gods and pay homage to Nebuchadnezzar. But as he lay drunk in his tent one night, Judith slipped in and cut off his head.

Good fortune smiled so readily upon *Antiochus* that he considered it possible for him to reach the stars. Out of his hatred for the Jews, he attempted to destroy them, but God sent down invisible pains upon him. In spite of the pain, he still proceeded to execute his plans. God then caused him to be crippled and made his body stink so badly that all people avoided him. Finally, he died a wretched and lonely death.

Alexander was so courageous that nothing could keep him from great deeds of valor and heroism. But eventually his own people turned against him and poisoned him.

Julius Caesar rose from a simple birth to become the mightiest man in the world. He was indeed blest with good fortune for a long time. But finally, even fickle fortune turned against him. Brutus and his cohorts stabbed Caesar to death, but even in death, Caesar remained a man as indicated by the way he covered himself with his cloak when he was dying.

The king of Lydia, *Croesus,* considered himself lucky after he was sentenced to death by fire and a heavy rain came and put out the fire. From there on, he thought himself immune to death. But he had a dream which was explained by his daughter as meaning that he would soon die by hanging.

Here the Knight interrupts the Monk.

Commentary

The Monk, unlike the Pardoner, will not permit himself the luxury of jest nor the undignified tale. Each of the Monk's stories is much like the others. It is not clear why Chaucer wrote these stories for the Monk. They are monotonous, and the inevitable moral of each comes as no surprise to the reader. Some authorities believe that Chaucer at one time considered writing a book of tragedies in the manner of Boccaccio. Indeed, Chaucer depended upon Boccaccio's work for his stories of Adam, Samson, Balthasar, Zenobia, Nero, and Croesus. Biblical narrative provided him with several of the other stories. His stories were sometimes incomplete, and Chaucer did not arrange them in chronological sequence; this perhaps accounts for the sense of whim and spontaneity of *The Monk's Tale.* Since Chaucer never completed his book of tragedies, it is believed that they are used in the *Canterbury Tales* simply because they were available and seemed suitable for the Monk to relate.

THE NUN'S PRIEST'S TALE: PROLOGUE

Summary

The Knight interrupts the Monk crying that his tales of woe are too much to bear. He asks the monk to tell a tale about a poor man who rises to good fortune. The Host agrees with the Knight and adds that the stories were so boring that he almost went to sleep. He entreats the Monk to tell a merry tale, but the Monk wants someone else to take a turn. The Host turns to the Nun's Priest and calls for a tale.

THE NUN'S PRIEST'S TALE

Summary
Once long ago in a small cottage near a meadow, the Nun's Priest began, there lived a widow and her two daughters. They had barely enough to keep them comfortable. Among her possessions was a cock called Chaunticleer. This rooster was a beautiful sight to behold, and nowhere in the land was there a cock who could match him in crowing. Chaunticleer was the master in some measure of seven hens. The loveliest of these was a beautiful and gracious hen named Lady Pertelote. She held the heart of Chaunticleer.

Now it so happened that one spring dawn as these birds sat on their perch, Chaunticleer began to groan and lurch. "'O dearest heart,/ What's ailing you?'" said Pertelote. Chaunticleer then recounted a terrible dream he had of a kind of beast or hound roaming in the yard trying to seize him. His color and marking were much the same as a fox.

"For Same," Pertelote said, "fye on you." She told him that it was cowardly to be afraid of dreams, and by showing such fear he has lost her love. She told him he dreamed because he ate too much and that no one should be afraid of dreams. It is well known that dreams have no meaning. She quotes Cato who says that dreams have no significance. Thus, she recommends a good laxative for Chaunticleer, and explains the relative value of each laxative. She even offers to prepare the cathartic, to be followed by a feast of choice worms.

Chaunticleer graciously thanks Pertelote, but he will quote a few authors who maintain that dreams have a very definite meaning. He recalled the story of two pilgrims who arrived in a busy town. There was a large crowd so they could not find lodging together. The first pilgrim found one room in an inn, but the second had to sleep in a nearby barn. During the night, the second pilgrim appeared to the first in a dream, saying that he was being murdered and crying for help. But the first pilgrim put this dream out of his mind and went back to sleep. Then in a second dream, the companion appeared again and said that the murderer was tossing his body in a dung cart which would be found at the city's gate the next morning. The next morning the companion arose and sought his friend in the barn. He was told that his friend was gone. The first pilgrim searched for the dung cart, and sure enough there was the body of his friend.

Chaunticleer then moralizes on murder, and is very pleased with his story, so pleased that he tells another one. Two men were to set sail the next day, but one dreamed that they were sure to be drowned and refused to go. His companion laughted at him for believing in dreams and went by himself. But as the ship was just a short distance out to sea, it sank and everyone was drowned.

Chaunticleer sees that his narration is affecting Pertelote, so he quotes several more authorities. He reminds her of St. Kenelm who saw his own murder in a dream. Furthermore, the *Dream of Scipio,* Daniel and Joseph's interpretation of dreams, and Andromache's dream should be remembered. And thus he ends his long speech with the conclusions that he needs no laxative.

Chaunticleer then felt that he had perhaps been too harsh on dear Pertelote, and he turns and compliments her on her looks and quotes to her the Latin phrase "In principio, mulier est hominis confusio" which he translates as "Woman is man's sole joy and bliss."

The Nun's Priest leaves Chaunticleer in his victory and pride with his seven ladies, and turns to the fox. This fox named Daun Russel has been hiding near the farmyard. The Nun's Priest now comments on traitors such as this fox, and compares him with such traitors as Judas and Ganelon. He follows this with a discussion of divine foreknowledge.

Returning to the plot, the Nun's Priest relates how Chaunticleer was watching a butterfly when he caught sight of the fox. He began immediately to run, but the fox called out in a gentle voice for Chaunticleer not to be afraid of a friend. He explains that he only came to hear Chaunticleer's beautiful voice. He maintains that he has only once before heard such a fine voice and that belonged to Chaunticleer's father. Now the fox wants to see if Chaunticleer can sing as well as his father could.

Thus, the vain cock shut his eyes and burst into song. At that moment the fox raced to the cock, grasped him about the neck, and made off with him. The hens in the barnyard made such a terrible commotion that they aroused the entire household. Soon the Widow, her two daughters, the dogs, hens, geese, ducks and even the bees were chasing the fox. It was so noisy that one would think the heavens were falling down.

Chaunticleer then says to the fox, "Why don't you turn around and throw a few insults at them." The fox thought this a good idea and as soon as he opened his mouth, Chaunticleer escaped and flew to a tree top. The fox tried to lure Chaunticleer down by compliments and sweet talk, but Chaunticleer had learned his lesson.

The Nun's Priest closes his tale by suggesting that his tale does have a moral.

Commentary

In *The Nun's Priest's Tale,* we have Chaucer at his best. Now, of course, animal stories are commonplace, and they have been a part of man's literature since earliest times. Perhaps Chaucer drew upon two similar fables, the French *Roman de Renard* and the German *Reinhart Fuchs.*

Nonetheless he improved upon these earlier stories by making his version much more real and much more interesting.

He did this by simply humanizing the rooster. Both the rooster and man have the same quality in common — vanity. The fox practices obvious flattery which is preeminently the quality of a tyrant.

Now if animals can talk, as indeed they do here, then they can dream and finally can discuss with great erudition the plausibility of dreams. Chaucer leads us charmingly through these stages in developing Chaunticleer, Pertelote, and the Fox into individuals suffering all the foibles of human nature. Yet never does Chaucer let us forget that these characters are but a cock, a hen, and a fox. For if we were to forget, the delicious humor of the story would be lost.

The reader should also remember that as the Priest is telling his story of Chaunticleer and his seven hens, the Priest is in a similar situation himself since he is the confessor to a group of nuns.

This tale is filled with many types of ironies. The reader should be aware of the human aspects of these barnyard creatures. Pertelote even refers to Chaunticleer's beard; yet in spite of their humanity they are nevertheless barnyard creatures. That they thus speak so learnedly and so nobly is an indirect comment on the absurdity of human aspirations.

The mock heroic tone should also be noted. The story is filled with classical allusions, with discussions about divine foreknowledge, and with a high moral tone. To offer a discussion of divine foreknowledge in the context of a barnyard chicken is the height of comic irony; that is, to have a foolish rooster being caught by a fox used as proof of divine foreknowledge is absurd. And to compare the plight of Chaunticleer to that of Homer's Hector and to suggest that the chase of the fox is an epic chase similar to classical epics indicates the absurdity of this situation.

It is likewise comic that Chaunticleer translates the Latin phrase incorrectly. He translates it as meaning that "woman is man's joy and bliss." But it actually means that woman is the downfall of man. And since Pertelote does not want to believe in Chaunticleer's dream, she is ironically contributing to his and ultimately her downfall.

THE SECOND NUN'S TALE: PROLOGUE

Summary

Idleness is a fiend that encourages vice and that fiend is forever laying a trap to catch people in his snare. Since Idleness is so dreadful, the Second Nun says she will follow her advice and get immediately down to the business of telling a tale. She offers to translate the life of St. Cecilia for the pilgrims.

The Second Nun offers an invocation to Mary. She asks for help in rendering accurately this tale of a maiden who remained true to her faith and conquered over the Devil. The Second Nun then praises the glories of Mary, the maid and mother. She asks forgiveness for possessing no more artistry with which to tell her tale.

The Second Nun now offers an *Interpretation of the Name Cecilia*. It means 1) heavenly lily for her chaste virginity; 2) the way for the blind by the example of her teachings; 3) holiness and busy-ness because of the derivation of the name from Latin; 4) wanting in blindness because of her clear virtues; and 5) heavenly because of the brightness of her works of excellence.

Commentary

Since Nuns in Chaucer's day were compelled to read stories of the saints, this is an apt selection for the Second Nun simply because she is a nun. Her invocation to Mary is typical for all stories, but more so here since the story of St. Cecilia is a story of chastity. And the interpretation of the name was a favorite device during Chaucer's day. Let it suffice here to say that the interpretation is not correct from an etymological viewpoint.

THE SECOND NUN'S TALE

Summary

There was once a noble young woman of Rome who loved chastity so much that she wanted to remain a virgin forever. But in time, she was given to a young man named Valerian in marriage. While the chapel bells were ringing for her wedding, she was praying to God to keep her chaste. That night after the wedding, she told her new husband that she had a guardian angel who would slay anyone who violated her body. Valerian asked to see the angel if he were to believe her. Cecilia tells him that he must first go to the Appian Way and there be baptised by Holy Urban.

Valerian went to Urban who rejoiced to see what power Cecilia had that she could convince a young man to be baptised. He praised God for Cecilia's chaste counsel. Suddenly, an old man appeared to them in a vision saying that there is one God and one faith and no more. Then the vision disappeared. But Valerian now believed and allowed himself to be baptized.

When he returned home, he found Cecilia with an angel holding a crown of lilies and a crown of roses. The angel said the crowns came from paradise, and no one will ever be able to see them unless he is chaste and hates villainy. The angel then grants Valerian a wish. Valerian explains that he has a brother whom he would like baptized into this great truth. But the brother, Tiburce, had objections. He did not want to be hunted for an outlaw as is Pope Urban. But when Cecilia explains that this life is not so important as the next, he asks other questions about the Christian faith which Cecilia carefully explained. Then Tiburce allowed himself to be baptized.

Later, an official named Almachius discovered the Christians, had them arrested and ordered them to sacrifice to the pagan gods. Supported by Cecilia, Valerian and Tiburce refused and were sentenced to death. Another official was so moved by their refusal that he became a Christian and was also executed.

When Cecilia was brought before the judge, he asked her many questions which she answered cleverly and wittily. She insults the pagan gods, and infers that Almachius is rather vain and ignorant. She is sentenced to death by being placed in heated water, but this fails. Then an executioner with a sword appeared and tried three times to cut off her head and did not completely succeed. Cecilia continued to live for three more days, converted more people to the church and finally died after willing her house to be made into a church. Pope Urban buried her body and proclaimed the house to be that of Saint Cecilia.

Commentary

Chaucer has repeated in *The Second Nun's Tale* an almost verbatim translation of an earlier and familiar Latin version. Despite the legend's improbabilities and use of the supernatural, the tale is filled with the noble spirit of high religion. Little is known of the historical Cecilia. Her martyrdom is assigned to the reign of Severus (A.D. 222-235).

THE CANON'S YEOMAN'S TALE: PROLOGUE

Summary

After the tale of Saint Cecilia, two men rode rapidly up to the pilgrims. One was judged to be a Canon by his black dress. The other was the Canon's Yeoman. Both seemed polite and the Host welcomed them and asked if either had a tale he could tell. The Yeoman answered immediately that his master knew lots about mirth and jollity. He then proceeded to tell about the Canon. They lived on the edges of towns and avoid the main roads. When asked why his face is so discolored, the Yeoman explained how he had to work with furnaces and fires, and his color is from his continually blowing. The Yeoman begins to tell the secrets of their trade, and all he knows about alchemy. The Canon attempts to stop him, but the Host will allow no threats. When the Canon sees that the Yeoman is going to tell everything, the Canon slips away in shame.

THE CANON'S YEOMAN'S TALE

Summary

PART I

Part one is actually a type of prologue where the Canon's Yeoman explains about their occupation and attempts at alchemy. He says that he is so deep in debt now that he will never be able to repay it all, and as a result of all his labors he has received this complexion and weak eyes. He explains about the various objects and equipment that they use in the practice of their craft. And everytime an experiment fails, the master tells him to begin again.

PART II

Once a Canon lived in London and practiced alchemy. He once borrowed a mark from a priest who reportedly had plenty of silver, and promised to return the mark in three days. The priest agreed but didn't expect to see his mark again. Therefore, he was very pleased when it was returned in three days. Furthermore, the Canon offered to reveal a couple of his discoveries. He sent for some quicksilver, and by tricks made the priest think that the quicksilver had been turned into real silver. The priest, not noticing the trick, was very pleased. The Canon then pretended to put an ingot of chalk into the fires, but he slipped a real ingot of silver in when the priest looked away. Again, the priest thought the chalk had been turned into silver. For a third time, the Canon filled a hollow stick with silver and plugged it with wax. When he placed it in the fire, the wax melted and silver poured forth. The beguiled priest wanted to buy the secret. The Canon asked for forty pounds and made the priest promise not to reveal the secrets to anyone. The Canon then promptly disappeared.

The remainder of the tale is an attack on the subject of alchemy and a conglomeration of all the ridiculous terms used by alchemists.

Commentary
The basic belief of alchemy involves the idea that certain baser metals lay in the ground for many years and ultimately become purer higher metals. The alchemist maintained that he could accelerate this process, and in a few moments time turn a base metal into a precious metal. This tale is not very popular with modern audiences because the entire concept of alchemy ceased to exist within a short period of time. But the alchemist made himself seem important by creating and using a very special set of terms. Then for the modern reader who does not know these terms and is not interested in learning them, the appeal of the story is limited.

THE MANCIPLE'S TALE: PROLOGUE

Summary
As the party moved on towards Canterbury, the Host noticed the Cook swaying in his saddle. The Cook was drunk and despite the Host's efforts to rouse him, he fell from his horse. The party of pilgrims halted and with great effort, the Cook was restored to his saddle. Then the Host turned to the Manciple and demanded a story.

THE MANCIPLE'S TALE

Summary

In a faraway land there lived a man named Phoebus. He was a great warrior, a skilled musician, very handsome, and kind. Phoebus had a wife whom he loved more than life itself. He bestowed upon her all the kindness and love at his command. But there was another side to Phoebus' character. He was extremely jealous.

Phoebus also kept in his house a marvelous, white-feathered crow which could repeat the words of anything he heard. Now it happened that Phoebus was called out of town. While he was gone, his wife's secret lover came to the home and made passionate love to her.

When Phoebus returned, the crow told him the scandalous sight he had seen. In a rage, Phoebus killed his wife. As his rage cooled, the sight of his wife's dead body brought on great remorse. In anger he turned to the crow and pulled all of its white feathers out and replaced them with black ones. And before throwing him out, he removed the crow's ability to sing and speak. The Manciple ends his tale by admonishing all people to restrain their tongues.

Commentary

The tale of the Manciple was short and simple. Its moral is clear: repeating scandal is a dangerous business. Chaucer also adds his own reflections on the futility of trying to restrain a wife. The author has simply retold here the long familiar tale of Apollo and Coronis in Ovid's *Metamorphoses*.

THE PARSON'S TALE: PROLOGUE

Summary

It was dusk and the pilgrims neared a small village. The Host turned to the last of the group, the Parson, and bid him tell his story and to be quick about it since it would soon be dark. The Parson said he was no rhymester, nor would he have a story that would amuse and entertain. Rather, he said, he had a sermon designed for those who wished to make the final mortal pilgrimage to the Heavenly Jerusalem.

THE PARSON'S TALE

Summary

God desires no man to perish, the Parson said, and there are many spiritual ways to the celestial city. One noble way is *Penitence,* the lamenting for sin, and the will to sin no more. The root of the tree of *Penitence* is *contrition;* the branches and the leaves are *confession;* the fruit, is *satisfaction;* the seed, is *grace;* and the heat in that seed is the *Love of God.*

Contrition, the Parson continued, is the heart's sorrow for sin. There are seven deadly sins, the first of which is *pride. Pride* takes many forms: arrogance, impudence, boasting, hypocrisy, and joy at having done someone harm. The remedy for *pride* is *humility.*

Envy is sorrow at the prosperity of others and joy in their hurt. The remedy for *envy* is to love God, your neighbor, your enemy.

Anger is the wicked will to vengeance. The remedy for *anger* is *patience.*

Sloth does all tasks with vexation, slackly, and without joy. The remedy is *fortitude.*

Avarice is the lecherous desire for earthy things. The remedy is *mercy.*

Gluttony is an immeasureable appetite for food and drink. The remedy is *abstinence, temperance,* and *sobriety.*

Lechery is theft. The remedy is *chastity* and *continence.*

Confession must be freely willed and made in good faith. It must be considered, and frequent.

Satisfaction consists in alms-giving, penance, fastings, and bodily pains. Its fruit is endless bliss in Heaven.

Commentary

It is rather obvious from the tales told by the pilgrims, and particularly by the eleven connected with the ecclesiastical organization, that the church of Chaucer's time had fallen upon evil days. It is fitting, therefore, that the tales should end on the high moral tone of the Parson's sermon. The original sermon, however, is a dreary and tiresome tract on the seven deadly sins that would have driven the ordinary parishioner from a church.

Scholars originally believed that *The Parson's Tale* was written by Chaucer. However, later research revealed that it was written from the work of two thirteenth-century Dominican friars. Indeed, so inartistic is Chaucer's writing here that some scholars believe that it was not Chaucer's work at all.

CHAUCER'S RETRACTIONS

The Maker of this Book here takes his Leave

Chaucer concluded his *Canterbury Tales* with a series of retractions. And if there be anything that displeases them, I beg them also to impute it to the fault of my want of ability, and not to my will, who would very gladly have said better if I had had the power. For our Books say 'all that is written is written for our doctrine'; and that is my intention. Wherefore I beseech you meekly for the mercy of God to pray for me, that Christ have mercy on me and forgive me for my sins: and especially for my translations and indictings of worldly vanities, which I revoke in my retractions: as are the book of *Troilus;* also the book of *Fame;* the book of *The Nineteen Ladies;* the book of *The Duchess;* the book of *St. Valentine's Day of the Parliament of Fowls; The Tales of Canterbury,...*and many another book, if they were in my memory; and many a song and many a lecherous lay; that Christ in his great mercy forgive me the sin.

Commentary

It is not clear why Chaucer wrote his retractions. Many wish that he had not. Perhaps the reason is that much of the *Canterbury Tales* was written at the zenith of his power and, in his latter days of sadness, he was seized by a poet's conscience. Scholars have puzzled over the retractions and conclude that perhaps we should not pry further into Chaucer's intentions here.

THE PRINCIPAL CHARACTERS

The principal characters of *The Canterbury Tales* are, of course, the twenty-nine members of the party of pilgrims who journeyed from London to the shrine of St. Thomas á Becket in Canterbury. While some of the tales told during the four-day journey certainly offer glimpses of Chaucer's life and times, the story tellers give an admirable view of fourteenth-century England as seen through the eyes of Chaucer.

A somewhat detailed description of each of the pilgrims is given in the Prologue (see its synopsis), but a complete listing will be repeated here.

Chaucer

The author (and our observer during the pilgrimage), who finally identifies himself.

The Knight

A distinguished soldier, gentleman, and idealist.

The Squire

The Knight's son, also a soldier of great valor, and a handsome young man filled with fire and enthusiasm.

The Yeoman
The servant of the Knight and the Squire, and also an expert bowsman.

The Nun
A graceful and mannerly Prioress who was "all sentiment and tender heart."

The Second Nun
Chaplain to the Prioress.

The Monk
An affluent priest who combined godliness and worldliness into a profitable and comfortable living.

The Friar
He was a Limiter which restricted his alms-begging to a certain district.

The Merchant
His forking beard and handsome dress, and his austere speech led all to believe him successful—which he was not.

The Oxford Cleric
Making a decent living was much less important to him than his study of books.

The Sergeant at the Law
An able lawyer who commanded good fees.

The Franklin
A land-owning Free Man, an epicure with adequate means to enjoy it.

The Haberdasher, Dyer, Carpenter, Weaver, and Carpet-maker
All guildsmen, impressively dressed, and obviously proud of their callings.

The Cook
He was the servant to the guildsmen and capable of making the finest dishes.

The Skipper
A good seaman, but a ruthless one.

The Doctor
Ably attended upon the sick, but not reluctant about charging a good fee.

The Woman of Bath
An excellent weaver, and a skilled wife who outlived her five husbands.

The Parson
A poor but honest cleric.

The Plowman
Honest workmen, faithful Christians, and unseemly charitable.

The Miller
A "great stout fellow" famous for his store of off-color stories but not noted for his honesty.

The Manciple
A steward for a college, noted as a shrewd buyer and running a debt-free school.

The Reeve
The successful manager of an estate, admired by his employers but feared by his employees.

The Summoner
His job—to summon sinners before the church court—condoned sin for a handsome bribe.

The Pardoner
His position (to offer indulgences or pardons of the Pope to sinners) were most often sold at handsome prices.

CRITICAL ANALYSIS

Geoffrey Chaucer is generally considered the Father of English poetry, and thus, one of the truly great men in our literature.

John Dyrden called him "the father of English poetry" and regarded him thusly:

[with the] same degree of veneration as the Grecians held Homer or the Romans held Virgil. He is a perpetual fountain of good sense, learned in all the sciences, and therefore speaks properly on all subjects: as he knew what to say, so he knows also to leave off, a habit which is practiced by few writers....

Coleridge looked at the poet this way:

I take unceasing delight in Chaucer. His cheerfulness is especially delicious to me in my old age. How exquisitely tender he is, and yet how perfectly free from the least touch of sickly melancholy or morbid drooping. The sympathy of the poet with the subjects of his poetry is particularly remarkable in Shakespeare and Chaucer; but what Shakespeare effects by a strong act of imagination and mental changing, Chaucer does without any effort, merely by the inborn kindly joyousness of his nature. How well we seem to know Chaucer! How absolutely nothing do we know of Shakespeare!

Yet it is a fact that somehow we have not realized the greatness of Chaucer, nor his genius. Perhaps a reason for this neglect lies in the difficulty and antiquity of his language. Yet an increasing number of modernized versions of his *Canterbury Tales* appear, and many of them preserve the essence of Chaucer's great art. There are, of course, many purists who believe there is no substitute for the original.

The student will note that in the commentary following each of the tales the origins of Chaucer's writings are attributed to other authors. It is indeed a fact that Chaucer owed a great debt to authors who went before him. Since virtually all of the tales are borrowed, what, one might ask, is properly Chaucer's own genius? The answer might be that nothing is left to Chaucer. Or the question might be answered that all is left to Chaucer!

Authors are seldom original. It is not the function of writers such as Chaucer to turn up something new under the sun. Rather, it is Chaucer's task to reassemble his material, give it fresh meaning, reveal new truths, commend new insights to his reader. In this sense, then, Chaucer was a remarkably original man.

Since Chaucer did give new meanings to twice-told tales, what was his purpose? Was he a great moral crusader? Do the *Canterbury Tales* offer new philosophic vistas?

Chaucer was a learned man. It is known that he read widely in French, Latin, and Italian. Yet it is rather remarkable that he did not write in the highly moralistic sense of the literary models he studied. He did not write in an abstract manner. He did not urge upon his readers new moralistic directions. *The Canterbury Tales* does not waft the reader to an exotic Oriental kingdom. He chose, instead, to set his story in the commonest sight of his time — a pilgrimmage to Canterbury. If Chaucer wished to create an illusion it was not of an imaginary world but of a real one. The tales of some of the pilgrims themselves *are* artificial forms but his real-life setting simply heightens the tales of some of the pilgrims.

When one considers the great scope of the *Tales*, perhaps the most consistent aspect of Chaucer's writing is its tremendous variety. Consider for a moment the brutally frank realism of *The Wife of Bath's Tale*, or the romance of *The Knight's Tale*, or the idealism of *The Prioress' Tale*, or the bawdiness of the Miller's Tale. But beyond the variety of Chaucer's tales, one is constantly reminded of Chaucer's humor. At one moment it is sly, at another moment, pure slapstick. But through it all, there is freshness and kindliness.

Chaucer, however, is capable of pathos and irony which sometimes blend as tragedy, sometimes as melodrama. As one reads Chaucer, the inescapable conclusion comes again and again that the great poet was forever concerned with the essential irony of human existence, with the rather ludicrous mockery arising from joy and ambition dashed unexpectedly by frustration and despair.

Chaucer's style is characterized chiefly by simplicity. Except in those cases where the author uses archaic form to preserve the rhyme effect, his words are commonplaces of ordinary people in ordinary circumstances. His sentences are simple in form and structure and noticeably free of studied balance. Indeed his writing is singularly free of the far-fetched puns and metaphors which characterize Shakespeare. To read Chaucer, then, is much like listening to a cultured and accomplished story teller. The tales tell themselves without effort or delay.

The device of a springtime pilgrimage, the diverse group of persons making up the company, and the adventures one can reasonably expect on such a journey, provided Chaucer with a wide range of characters and experiences. The setting does not permit boredom. We are told in the Prologue that each member of the company was to tell two stories. This would have amounted to sixty tales, plus the author's account of the stay in Canterbury. All of which brings us around to another aspect of *The Canterbury Tales*.

What we have today are, in reality, fragments. Chaucer had intended a much more ambitious undertaking which surely would have exceeded in length Boccaccio's famous *Decameron*. Chaucer's scheme never materialized and what survives is one fourth of his original proposal. There is not even one tale from each pilgrim, nor are there connecting links (between many of the tales) which would have given greater unity to Chaucer's work. Chaucer did not leave for posterity the order in which the tales were to be told beyond *The Prologue* and *The Knight's Tale*, at the beginning, and *The Parson's Tale* at the close.

Of all of the tales in this work, surely the greatest of them is *The Prologue*. Here Chaucer gives an accounting of human life as he viewed it in medieval England. Every phase of life in England is represented, except royalty. This, it may be added, is the truly original work of Chaucer, for nothing like it prior to Chaucer's time has ever been discovered.

The gay, bouyant, good-natured *Prologue,* however, contrasts sharply with the ending of the tales. In *The Prologue* and throughout the telling of the tales, the members of the company are repeatedly urged by the Host to tell humorous and interesting tales. But *The Parson's Tale,* and more strikingly, Chaucer's Retractions, offer the totally new note of disavowing pleasure, story-telling, and sensuousness. "Let us repent," Chaucer cries, "and beg the mercy of God."

Chaucer must have been a good churchman or he would have lost his favors from the Court. His writings, it must be remembered, were aimed at satirizing or exposing only individuals. Matters of doctrine were never attacked by Chaucer. And so Chaucer, who had composed one of the great classics of English literature in a largely playful mood, embracing and enjoying all the foibles of human nature, closes his great work with a grim supplication for heavenly forbearance.

QUESTIONS FOR EXAMINATION AND REVIEW

Note: The section or sections indicated in parenthesis following each question contain information which will help you answer the question.

1. How did Geoffrey Chaucer differ from other writers of his time in the English Middle Ages? (See Sketch of Chaucer's Life and Times.)

2. What in your opinion was the underlying motive for the tale told by the Wife of Bath? (See Synopsis.)

3. If you were asked to single out the most persistent aspect of Chaucer's style in the *Canterbury Tales,* what in your opinion would it be? Why? (See Critical Analysis.) What is the major strength of his style?

4. Some critics have held that Chaucer had embraced the early spirit of Wycliffe's Reformation and therefore was against the established Roman Church. Do you agree? (See Critical Analysis, and Synopsis of the Author's Retractions.)

5. Many believe that the most important single part of *The Canterbury Tales* is *The Prologue.* What is the basis for this judgment? (See Critical Analysis.)

6. When is it assumed that Chaucer began writing his *Canterbury Tales* and when did he stop work on them? (See Sketch of the Author's Life and Times.)

7. How many pilgrims started the journey to Canterbury? How was it determined who should tell stories while the party was enroute? (See Synopsis of *Prologue*.)

8. What is the importance of *The Canterbury Tales* to the social historian? (See Critical Analysis.)

9. Which character occupies the central position among the pilgrims as they near their destination? (See Synopsis, *The Parson's Tale*.)

10. Define and illustrate at least five literary forms used by Chaucer in the *Tales*. (See Middle English Literary Genres.)

11. What is the function of the final chapter of the Boo ? (See Critical Analysis and Synopsis.)

12. How complete is Chaucer's description of England in the Fourteenth Century? (See Sketch of Author's Life and Times, and the Critical Analysis.)

13. Who are the chief characters in the Pilgrimage? Identify and briefly characterize each. (See Synopsis of the *Prologue,* and the Characters.)

14. If you were asked to select the best tale told during the journey to Canterbury which would it be? Why?

15. What reason is advanced for the fact that Chaucer's *Canterbury Tales* has not been as widely read as, for example, some of Shakespeare's plays? (See Critical Analysis.)

16. What position has Chaucer been assigned in the history of English literature? (See Introduction.)

17. What role does realism play in Chaucer's writings? (See Critical Analysis.)

18. Critics claim that precious little of Chaucer's writings were original; that is, that he borrowed from others for his tales. Discuss. (See Critical Analysis.)

19. Describe briefly life in England during Chaucer's time. (See Sketch of Author's Life and Times.)

20. Discuss Chaucer as a humorist or a satirist. Is he obvious or subtle? Is he kind or critical? Is he coarse? Is he merry? (Develop your own ideas here.)

21. Select your favorite person on the journey to Canterbury. Describe him or her in detail. Select and describe your favorite character from one of the tales. (Develop your own ideas here.)

22. Which of the Tales interested you the most? Which Tale seemed the most artistically conceived of the whole group? (Again develop your own ideas.)

FOR FURTHER READING: A SELECT BIBLIOGRAPHY

Bowden, Muriel, *A Commentary on the General Prologue to The Canterbury Tales,* New York: Macmillan Co., 1948.

Chute, Marchette G., *Geoffrey Chaucer of England,* New York: Dutton, 1946.

Coghill, Nevill, *The Canterbury Tales,* Baltimore: Penguin Books, 1952.

Coghill, Nevill, *The Poet Chaucer,* Oxford: Oxford University Press, 1949.

French, Robert D., *A Chaucer Handbook,* New York: Appleton-Century-Crofts, 1947.

Hitchins, H. L., *The Canterbury Tales,* London: John Murray, 1947.

Kennedy's *Concordance of Chaucer.*

Kluge, Freidrich, *The Language and Meter of Chaucer,* New York: Macmillan Co., 1915.

Kittredge, G. L., *Chaucer and His Poetry,* Cambridge: Harvard University Press, 1901.

Lloyd, J. L., *A Chaucer Selection,* London: George C. Harrop, 1952.

Lowes, John Livingston, *Geoffrey Chaucer and the Development of His Genius,* Boston: Houghton-Mifflin Co., 1934.

Lumiensky, M. R., *The Canterbury Tales,* London: John Murray Ltd, 1948.

Malone, Kemp, *Chapters on Chaucer,* Baltimore: Johns Hopkins University Press, 1951.

Manly, J. M., *Canterbury Tales,* New York: Holt, 1930.

Moody, William Vaughn, and Lovett, Robert Morss, *A History of English Literature,* New, York: Charles Scribner's Sons, 1946.

Morrison, Theodore, *The Portable Chaucer,* New York: The Viking Press, 1949.

Owens, Charles A. Jr., *Discussions of the Canterbury Tales,* Boston: D. C. Heath, 1961.

Spurgeon, C. F. E., *Five Hundred Years of Chaucer Criticism and Allusion, 1357-1900.* Chaucer Society, 7 parts, 1914-1924; also 3 volumes, Cambridge, 1925; Supplement, London, 1920.

Vickers, K. H., *England in the Later Middle Ages,* New York: Putnam, 1919.

Your Guides to Successful Test Preparation.

Cliffs Test Preparation Guides

Efficient preparation means better test scores. Go with the experts and use **Cliffs Test Preparation Guides.** They'll help you reach your goals because they're: Complete • Concise • Functional • In-depth. They are focused on helping you know what to expect from each test. The test-taking techniques have been proven in classroom programs nationwide.

Recommended for individual use or as a part of formal test preparation programs.

TITLES		QTY.
2068-8	**ENHANCED ACT ($5.95)**	
2030-0	**CBEST ($7.95)**	
2040-8	**CLAST ($8.95)**	
1471-8	**ESSAY EXAM ($4.95)**	
2031-9	**ELM Review ($6.95)**	
2060-2	**GMAT ($7.95)**	
2008-4	**GRE ($6.95)**	
2065-3	**LSAT ($7.95)**	
2033-5	**MATH Review for Standardized Tests ($8.95)**	
2017-3	**NTE Core Battery ($14.95)**	
2020-3	**Memory Power for Exams ($4.95)**	
2044-0	**Police Sergeant Examination Preparation Guide ($9.95)**	
2032-7	**PPST ($7.95)**	
2002-5	**PSAT/NMSQT ($4.50)**	
2000-9	**SAT ($5.95)**	
2042-4	**TASP ($7.95)**	
2018-1	**TOEFL w/cassette ($14.95)**	
2034-3	**VERBAL Review for Standardized Tests ($7.95)**	
2041-6	**You Can Pass the GED ($9.95)**	

Prices subject to change without notice.

Available at your local bookseller or order by sending the coupon with your check. **Cliffs Notes, Inc., P.O. Box 80728, Lincoln, NE 68501.**

Name _____

Address _____

City _____

State _____ Zip_____

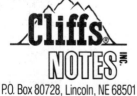

P.O. Box 80728, Lincoln, NE 68501